MW00356589

living LIGHTS
shining STARS

living LIGHTS *shining* STARS

Ten Secrets to Becoming the Light of theWorld

DR. M. NORVEL YOUNG

with Mary Hollingsworth

HOWARD
PUBLISHING CO.
West Monroe, Louisiana

Our purpose at Howard Publishing is to:

- *Increase faith* in the hearts of growing Christians
- *Inspire holiness* in the lives of believers
- *Instill hope* in the hearts of struggling people everywhere

Because He's coming again

Living Lights, Shining Starts
© 1997 by Dr. M. Norvel Young, 24255 Pacific Coast Highway, Malibu, CA 90263-4507. Administered by Mary Hollingsworth, Shady Oaks Studio, 1507 Shirley Way, Fort Worth, TX 76022. All rights reserved.
Printed in the United States of America

Published by Howard Publishing Co., Inc.,
3117 North 7th Street, West Monroe, Louisiana 71291-2227

No part of this publication may be reproduced in any form without the prior written permission of the publisher except in the case of brief quotations within critical articles and reviews.

Library of Congress Cataloging-in-Publication Data

Young, M. Norvel (Matt Norvel), 1915-
    Living lights, shining stars : ten secrets to becoming the light of the world / by M. Norvel Young ; with Mary Hollingsworth.
        p.   cm.
    Includes bibliographical references.
    ISBN 1-878990-76-4
    1. Christian life.   2. Christian ethics.   I. Hollingsworth, Mary, 1947-   . II. Title.
    BV4501.2.Y664   1997
    248.4--dc21
                                                                97-25096
                                                                CIP

Cover design by LinDee Loveland

Unless otherwise noted, Scriptures quoted from The Holy Bible, New Century Version, copyright © 1991 by Word Publishing, Dallas, Texas 75039. Used by permission.

DEDICATION

✧

To the women in my life:

Ruby Morrow Young
Irene Young Mattox
Emily Young Lemley
Marilyn Young Stewart
Sara Young Jackson
and
Helen Mattox Young

"You are the light . . . be a light for other people. Live so that they will see the good things you do and will praise your Father in heaven."

Matthew 5:14, 16

✧

"Shine like stars in the dark world. You offer the teaching that gives life."

Philippians 2:15–16

C O N T E N T S

✧

CONTENTS

CHAPTER 4

What's the Good Word?

The Power of Good in Communication

An Inspirational Message from Dr. Paul Faulkner

❖ 67 ❖

CHAPTER 5

Making Good Grades

The Power of Good in Education

An Inspirational Message from Dr. R. Gerald Turner

❖ 87 ❖

CHAPTER 6

Good Morning, Darling

The Power of Good in Your Family

An Inspirational Message from Dr. H. Norman Wright

❖ 107 ❖

CHAPTER 7

As Good As Gold

The Power of Money Used for Good

An Inspirational Message from Dr. Ronald J. Sider

❖ 127 ❖

ACKNOWLEDGMENTS

✧

No book is ever published by one person, and this one is a testimony to that fact. If it had been up to me alone, it would never have happened. Here are some important contributors to the book and to my life, neither of which would be as rich without them:

- *Helen.* As always, she served as my partner, support, and constant encouragement in every aspect of the book. Nothing much happens in my life without her. Thank you, Helen.

- *Mary Hollingsworth.* It has been a gratifying experience working with my dear friend as the coauthor. Thank you, Mary. You've carried the burden, and I love you.

- *Howard Publishing Company.* I owe sincerest appreciation to the great people at Howard. Their commitment to us is humbling. Thank you, Howard.

- *Gloria Drass.* Without this talented woman, the book would still be a large box full of articles, raw research, and magazines. Thank you, Gloria.

- *Contributors.* So many wonderful people have given their blessings to this book with chapter-opening comments, endorsements, and the Foreword. To each of these we say a heartfelt thank you: Bill Bright, Bill Banowsky, Paul Faulkner, Ruth Peale, Mother Teresa, Robert Seiple, Joni Eareckson Tada, Gerald Turner, H. Norman Wright, Ronald Sider, and Richard Mouw.

F O R E W O R D

✧

Dr. Norvel Young has played a major role in helping to build one of the truly great universities of our time, Pepperdine University. He has dedicated his life to training tens of thousands of students to shine like stars in a dark universe.

From over fifty years of reading thousands of books and booklets, I can truthfully say from broad experience that he has written one of the most refreshing and positive books I have ever discovered! It contains a wonderfully constructive message, delightfully sprinkled with numerous fascinating anecdotes and examples.

We are so bombarded with all the negatives in this world, we sometimes pay too much attention to them and forget that our assignment in this life is to emulate our wonderful Lord, who spent his time "doing good." The Scriptures tell us that Jesus was "anointed with the Holy Spirit and power, and went around doing good" (Acts 10:28).

"Doing good" was his mission. In describing his purpose, the Lord quoted the prophecy about him, which Isaiah wrote hundreds of years earlier: "The Spirit of the Lord is on me, because he has anointed me to preach good news to the poor. He has sent me to proclaim freedom for the prisoners and recovery of sight for the blind, to release the oppressed, to proclaim the year of the Lord's favor" (Luke 4:18–19).

By God's grace and gift, Spirit-filled believers are also "anointed with the Holy Spirit and power." Since we are ambassadors for Christ, and since he lives within us, he wants to live his life through us. By the enabling Holy Spirit, the Lord desires us to be channels of his goodness and blessings to others in a world filled with darkness and gloom, heartache and sorrow.

This does not mean just preaching the good news or sharing the saving gospel message with them, although this is of supreme importance. But by our words and deeds, often in just little ways, we can also often bring freedom to those who are captive to the evil mindsets of this world and bring release or relief to those oppressed by its effects.

With great insight and sensitivity, Dr. Young helps us understand how to do good in all aspects of life, including our thoughts, our words, our families, our communities, and other important areas. Instead of focusing on the darkness, he helps us focus on the positive things of life, as we are exhorted by the Holy Spirit through the apostle Paul: "Finally, brothers, whatever is true, whatever is noble, whatever is right, whatever is pure, whatever is lovely, whatever is admirable—if anything is excellent or praiseworthy—think about such things" (Philippians. 4:8).

Bill Bright
Founder and President,
Campus Crusade for Christ International

PREFACE

✦

An ancient Chinese proverb says, "It is better to light one candle than to curse the darkness." These words, which have been heard around the world, contain a profound truth, as well as practical advice.

You and I have seen the power of an individual to effect change. As a tiny flame illuminates the darkness, so we have seen even the simplest kindness change the atmosphere in an elevator, a meeting room, or a family, and thus contribute to a better world.

It's tempting for all of us at times to simply gripe about the problems, to surrender to discouragement, or to allow the everyday pressures of our own schedules to consume all of our time and energy; and we may say, "Let George do it." But the truth is: *We are George.* So, we ask ourselves, "If not by me, by whom? If not now, when?" Edmund Burke, the eighteenth-century statesman was right when he said, "The only thing necessary for the triumph of evil is for good men to do nothing."

Only One

My dear friend, Blanche Seaver, who is responsible more than any other individual for the financial strength of Pepperdine University, where I serve as chancellor emeritus, used to give a brief message to the graduates at each commencement exercise of our Frank Roger Seaver College. She often closed her remarks with these powerful words from Edward Everett Hale:

> I am only one.
> But still I am one.
> I cannot do everything,
> But still I can do something.
> And because I cannot do everything,
> I will not refuse to do the something
> that I can do.

Of all the people I have known, Blanche Seaver did the something she could do. She practiced what she preached. She and her husband were deeply committed to our country. They worked tirelessly for good government. Frank wrote the Los Angeles County charter. Blanche supported candidates at every level, from mayor to president. But her great love was young people.

She believed, "If I want to do something for the good of our country, then I'll help the youth of our country, for they are its future." And because she could not do everything, she didn't fail to do all she could. She was indefatigable in doing good. And her one candle burned brightly in the darkness.

I think of determination and perseverance when I think of Blanche Seaver. These are a part of any formula for success. They are the real fuels of accomplishment. Dietrich Bonhoeffer, who defied the Nazis and gave his life for his faith, said, "Action springs not from thought, but from a readiness for responsibility." When you and I accept responsibility to make a difference for good in our own families, our own churches, our own communities, offices, or schools, we will change the world to the degree that we accept that responsibility. You don't have to get your name in the paper, write a bestseller, or be on television to light candles of goodness by constructive action.

Here Come the Good Guys

In his 1996 bestseller, *Slouching towards Gomorrah,* author Robert H. Bork describes the problem of darkness and evil well. We need to know these facts, it's true. But I agree with Christian leader Tony Evans, who says, "The job of light is to shine, not to analyze the darkness." We can join the Chicken Littles and the gloom-and-doomers, or we can light candles. That's the choice.

I've seen the hideous power of evil and the devastation it can cause, as you will discover throughout this book, but I've made my choice—I prefer to shine, as a reflection of the light, rather than analyze. I want to refract the light of God in all its glorious colors into the dark corners of my own life and the lives of others.

I believe that if we look for the good in life, we'll find it. Most people are just good, ordinary folks, living their lives one day at a time. They go to work, do the best job they can, and come home to take care of their families. Many of them go to church, help with community improvement, vote on a fairly regular basis, and pay their debts. They volunteer with the Little League or help a neighbor build a new fence. They don't go out barhopping, rioting, robbing convenience stores, or stripping cars. They're good, decent people who are frightened by the barrage of news about evil and its terrorist activities.

These are the millions of law-abiding citizens whose internal strength of character and well-trained consciences can light candles in the darkness they fear. This is the huge silent majority, who quietly withdraw from evil into the refuge of their homes but who have the awesome power of good at their disposal, if they will but energize it with proactive good deeds. These are the people who need to rise up, bringing the power of their lights together, and as a huge unified force, chase evil back into the shadows. These people are you and me, our families, friends, and neighbors.

The Right Time

In truth, there are wonderful people all over our country lighting candles in the darkness—doing good—not because they *have* to but because they want their world to be a better place. Good is an awesome power. When that power is unleashed, when it becomes bold instead of timid, evil tucks its tail and runs for cover.

Only through the unleashing of good can evil be chased into hiding. And it's time! Time for us to *do* good. Time for us to be actively good, not just passively good. Time for us to be boldly good, not just timidly good. Time for us to be aggressively good, not just anemically good. It's time to grab evil by the nape of the neck and the seat of the pants and toss it out into the darkness where it belongs.

Unfortunately, we've been fed a lie for decades. We've been told that it's not cool to be goody-goody. We've been told that everybody has a little larceny in their hearts—it's natural. We've been convinced to keep quiet about our religion, our morals, and our ethics in order to be tolerant or to keep our jobs. Society says, "Live and let live," "Mind your own business," "Leave well enough alone," "Don't get involved." But have you ever pondered whether these concepts are from God?

And as a result of this hands-off philosophy, evil romps freely through our lives, leaving death and destruction in its wake, while good is often chained in the dungeon of our fears. Meanwhile, we curse the darkness. We analyze, but we don't shine.

The most marvelous story of active good in all literature is the story of a man of a racial minority who encountered a man of another race in a ditch, beaten and bleeding. Without a social-service agency or friends or relatives to help, the wounded man would have died. But the man we call the Good Samaritan had the light of compassion burning in his heart. Alone, with no one to applaud his good deed, he provided transportation, medical attention, a hotel, and a first-century credit card to help his *enemy*. His brilliant example reminds us that one individual with love in his heart is the greatest force for good in the world.

Our Good Purpose

I believe God has put each of us in this world for good purposes—personal missions in life that we alone can accomplish. And if we don't do them, those jobs will remain undone. I have my mission. With God's help, I want to light as many candles of faith and hope as possible to make this a better world. I want to be like Jesus, who went everywhere doing good.

"It is better to light one candle than to curse the darkness. Good always dispels evil." This book will help you light candles of goodness in at least ten ways. It will help you defend yourself against Satan using God's secret weapon—the awesome power of doing good.

Am I suggesting a quick fix? No. Is it a simple, once-for-all-time act? No. You know how candles are—after a while, they burn down and must be replaced with new ones. But wherever and whenever candles of goodness burn, the darkness of evil is dispelled. The more candles you light, one by one, the farther away darkness is driven.

It's time! Time for us to get out of our recliners and begin lighting candles. My hope is for the light of good to glow brightly in your life . . . but only you can light the flame. Don't let the candle-quenchers of cynicism and despair blow out your candle. "Do not let evil defeat you, but defeat evil by doing good" (Romans 12:21).

CHAPTER ONE

Never Underestimate the Power of Good

secret

No. 1 – Purposely shine the light of aggressive goodness into every dark corner of the world.

Mother Teresa
Serving the poor in Calcutta, India

We don't need to worry about why problems exist in the world. We just need to respond to people's needs. We must try to give unconditionally whatever each person needs at that moment. The point is to do something, however small, and show you care by giving your time. I'm just so thankful to be able to help the poor.

Good people can look forward to a bright future,
but the future of the wicked is like a flame going out.

Proverbs 13:9

The Power of Aggressive Good

The wind-whipped fire was raging out of control, galloping
across Los Angeles County, charring homes, lives, and
businesses as it went. The beautiful Malibu campus of
Pepperdine University was trapped in the middle of the
engulfing smoke and flames, like a terrified camper encircled by
howling wolves in the night. Thousands of firefighters were working furiously. Helicopters carrying tons of water dropped their cargo
and quickly circled to return for another load.

Hundreds of people had already lost their homes to the fire, and
the houses on Tiner Court, where we live, were being evacuated. My
wife, Helen, and I had been watching the news reports on television
in our room in the Holiday Inn Crown Plaza in Bangkok, Thailand,
where we were staying. We were praying constantly that homes and
lives would be spared.

About six o'clock that evening, we quietly dressed for dinner and went to the lobby to meet one of our Pepperdine alumni. Kumar Harilela, our host at the hotel, met us with a reserved smile, sharing our concern.

"Before we go to dinner, I have someone I'd like you to meet," he said. "This guest has been in the hotel for a week or so, resting."

We agreed and followed Kumar into the elevator. We arrived on the top floor and walked down the hall past the presidential suite, where Kumar had insisted we stay, to one of the single rooms at the end. He knocked quietly on the door and stepped back.

✧

"I'm just so thankful to be able to help the poor."

✧

The door opened, and there stood . . . Mother Teresa! I was surprised; I was thrilled; I was humbled. She smiled warmly and invited us in. We spent a precious half-hour with Mother Teresa hearing about her work and answering her questions about ours. One comment she made stuck with me especially. She said, "I'm just so thankful to be able to help the poor."

She asked about Pepperdine and said she had been watching the fire and praying for those in danger. Then she took my right hand and said, "You remember the words of Jesus, 'Inasmuch as you do it unto the least of these my brethren . . .' " She paused, then completed Jesus' statement as she pointed to each of my five fingers in turn, "You do it unto me." I'll never forget the inspirational example of her life of service or her five-finger sermon. To do good to the lowliest is to serve the Lord Christ.

We came away from that small room amazed at her humility and quiet confidence. As we walked down the hall, back toward the elevator, I asked Kumar, "Why didn't you put *her* in the presidential suite?"

"I tried to, but she didn't feel that she deserved it."

I've thought of her selflessness often in the past months. What incredible influence this fragile-looking woman wields! What respect she has garnered from around the world. And why?

She hasn't discovered a cure for cancer. She didn't invent the Internet or the World Wide Web. She's not a great orator or government leader. She hasn't written a *New York Times* bestseller, produced a blockbuster movie, or composed a masterpiece. She's not even physically commanding. So why is she one of the most admired women in the world? What makes her so special?

Doing good. Day after day Mother Teresa does good in the name of Christ. She helps the poorest of the poor. She works to relieve the pain and suffering of the dying she sees around her. She has dedicated her life to doing good. That's all. And people everywhere want to be like her.

Goodness exudes from Mother Teresa. Her gentleness and love for people are not just good qualities; they extend to what she *does.* She simply does what good she can, and her goodness is multiplied by others trying to emulate her. Talk about a living light! I wonder how many other candles have been lit from her flame?

People often lament over not doing something important. They want to impact society in some grandiose way—solve national and international problems—but they say in defeat, "I'm just one person; what good can I do?"

Mother Teresa is just one person . . . doing the good she sees to do around her. She lights a candle in the darkness by feeding one hungry child, another one by providing a coat to a widow whose clothes are in tatters, and yet another by giving medicine to a suffering man. These simple acts of goodness, repeated from day to day, have ignited enough candlepower to bring the light of hope to a starving world.

But she's extraordinary, you say. *I could never be like her.*

Helen and I didn't find her to be extraordinary. In fact, she met us at the door in her bare feet and her simple habit. She's actually a very simple, ordinary woman, whose passion in life is to do good.

These words, spoken by Adlai Stevenson of Eleanor Roosevelt, aptly describe Mother Teresa: "her glow has warmed the world."

She reminds me of the widow in Luke 21 who gave two half-cent coins to God. Jesus didn't criticize her for doing so little; he praised her for doing so much. She did all that she could, and that pleased him greatly. And that's what Mother Teresa does. We should never underestimate the incredible power that a small act of goodness can have.

Aggressive Good

The first "secret" to becoming the light of the world is to become aggressive in doing good. Like Mother Teresa, our love for others must find expression in actions. The term *aggressively good* is an oxymoron. (What's an oxymoron? It's two seemingly contradictory terms that, when combined, create a whole new meaning, like servant leadership or deafening silence.) The word *aggressive* has fallen into disrepute in recent years and taken on a negative connotation, that is, unless we need it for something important. We still want our military to be aggressive against terrorists like Saddam Hussein. We still like aggressive salespeople . . . when they work for us. And we want aggressive sports teams, so we can be on the winning side.

What we don't like are *obnoxious* aggressive people. So, today we prefer to be called *assertive*, which is supposedly a kinder, gentler term than *aggressive*. But, if we're going to win the war against aggressive evil, we've got to be more than nicely assertive. We have to quit playing footsie with the enemy. We also have to be aggressive, in the military sense. We've got to be aggressive, like a successful insurance salesman. We've got to be as aggressive as a professional football team that's twenty points behind in the fourth quarter. But we have to be aggressively good.

Of Candles and Lighthouses

I once heard Helen Keller speak to the state legislature of Tennessee. Her face was radiant with enthusiasm and earnestness. She said that in her youth she had longed to do great things, but she could not. So she decided to do small things in a great way. She put her heart into doing the good she could where she was with what she had. And her life was a bright light, even though she lived in her own dark world.

Have you ever wondered what the world would be like if there were more than one Mother Teresa? Or more than one Helen Keller? What if there were two? What if there were ten? Or a hundred? There would be a bonfire of candlepower! The light of good would be staggering—like the brilliance of Times Square on New Year's Eve! And evil would be stampeded into a small dark closet where it would cower from the light.

✧

Perhaps there *are* more Mother Teresas in our world—people who go through life doing good. Quiet people who don't make a lot of noise about the good they do. Ordinary people all around us who are lighting candles in the darkness, one by one. After all, a candle loses none of its light by lighting another candle. The candle we light with constructive action may ignite another candle, while losing none of its own brilliance.

There is no competition between lighthouses.

✧

Through the years I have often said, "There is no competition between lighthouses." We should encourage every good work and never sink to jealousy or a competitive spirit. There's so much need for good in this world, we'll never have too many candles or lighthouses.

Good's Irresistible Power

It was the early seventies, and Cambodia, in the words of Stan Mooneyham—former president of World Vision—was "aflame with the war" that had engulfed Southeast Asia. Tranquil Phnom Penh had become a fetid, sprawling refugee camp. The call went out for humanitarian assistance, but only a few good-hearted people responded to the unpopular cause.

Stan Mooneyham was one of them. At great personal risk, he led a small caravan with ten tons of relief supplies across a bombed-out highway plagued by thievery and rebel ambush. Cambodia's government held no love for Christianity; but World Vision's caravan made it through, and Mooneyham was invited to return to Cambodia some time later to preach. Little did anyone know at the time that the Christian movement then gaining momentum would, in a few short years, be ground underfoot by Pol Pot in Cambodia's infamous killing fields.

❖

"Love talked about can be easily turned aside, but love demonstrated is irresistible."

❖

Among those sitting and listening to Mooneyham was a Communist spy, a young man named Sovann. As he heard the translator relay the story of the prodigal son, his heart was gripped. He listened as Stan taught that, "Love talked about can be easily turned aside, but love demonstrated is irresistible." When the Khmer Rouge over-ran Cambodia, Sovann was caught in a prayer meeting with World Vision staff and arrested. Narrowly escaping death, he spent years as a prisoner, then as a refugee. He finally returned to Cambodia to preach reconciliation.

Sovann adopted the name "Barnabas" during his years with the underground church. He's now a faithful worker in Cambodia, who thinks of himself only as a humble tool in the hands of a gracious

8

God. His infectious smile and gracious speech are an amazing testimony to the irresistible power of aggressive good.

There are Helen Kellers, Stan Mooneyhams, and Mother Teresas all over the world—good people with hearts full of kindness, love, and hope, people who inspire *us* to do good too, people who let us light our flickering candles from their steady flames.

The truth is, good multiplies into greater good. In every area of life, if good is applied, greater good will usually result—from health, to the family, to education, to the media. And so it is. Good promotes good.

Good to His Robbers

Once, the father of Immanuel Kant, the great philosopher, made a perilous trek through the forests of Poland to his native country of Silesia. On the road the old man was accosted by a band of thieves, who demanded all his valuables. Then they asked, "Have you given us all?" He was only allowed to leave when he had answered, "Yes, all."

Finally reaching safety out of their sight, Kant stopped to rest. As he sat down, his hand touched something hard in the hem of his robe. It was his gold! He had sewn it there for safety and had quite forgotten it in his fear and confusion with the robbers.

Kant at once hurried back to find the thieves. When he found them, he said meekly, "I have told you what was not true. It was unintentional. I was too terrified to think. Here, take the gold in my robe."

To the old man's utter surprise, the robbers refused his gold. Then one thief went to his saddlebags and brought back Kant's stolen purse and gave it to him. Another robber gave him back his book of prayer, while the last one led Kant's stolen horse to him and helped him mount it.

The final surprise came when all three robbers asked Kant for his forgiveness and blessing, which he gave. Then they watched him slowly ride away. Goodness had triumphed over evil.

Looking for the Good

Isn't it sad when society deteriorates into being surprised by someone who simply does what's right? Today we're no longer shocked by cruelty, injustice, cynicism, rape, abuse, murder, racial hatred, or other forms of despicable evil. Instead, we're surprised by honesty, kindness, generosity, goodness, and outpourings of love and concern. We are starved for words of encouragement and hope. We long for truthful politicians who keep their promises and preachers who practice what they preach. We dream of "the *good* old days" when neighbors took care of each other and we could sleep peacefully with all the doors unlocked.

Let's not focus on what's *wrong* and overlook all that's *right* around us. Let's look at the donut instead of the hole. There's so much good in our world. Did you know that every week more Americans attend church services than the total number of fans at all the sporting events in America for a whole year? That's good!

Every year Americans willingly contribute millions of dollars to organizations that do good things for people. And as the government shrinks its assistance to such programs, as it will with the new welfare program, volunteer givers have to take up the slack.

Happy volunteers donate millions of hours in service to others at hospitals, counseling centers, hospices, shelters, and schools. In 1996 alone, over 93 million Americans did volunteer work for nonprofit organizations, according to the U.S. Bureau of Statistics. In fact, 50 percent of American adults volunteer an average of four hours per week to some worthwhile cause. That's really good! Our society functions because of unselfish donors and willing volunteers.

Let's focus on dedicated teachers and school administrators who give their whole lives to prepare young people as good citizens and productive people, even when some students bring guns to school and police have to stand guard in the halls to protect those teachers from the very students they are determined to help. These are not ordinary people; these are *fantastic* people doing enormous good!

Think about volunteers who teach immigrants to read and write English so they can function well in their new homeland. And remember the thousands of missionaries who sacrifice "the good life" at home for lives of poverty and hardship to meet the desperate spiritual needs of others abroad. There is so much that is so good.

I believe there's a resurgence of goodness and morality in our country, which will hopefully wash America clean. Fathers are getting back to the business of parenting. More and more women are finding joy in staying home with their small children. The silent majority is beginning to speak out against immorality, crime, and corruption. Some television executives are striving to produce more family-oriented programs.

The tide is definitely turning. And good will ride the wave, while evil is pulled out to sea in the undertow. I believe there are days ahead of returning hope and goodness.

I'm so certain of it myself that I've already begun issuing invitations to a New Year's Eve party to celebrate the new millennium on January 1, 2000, in the Firestone Fieldhouse of Pepperdine University. I'm more excited about the future and the opportunities for good it offers than ever before. *It's great to be alive!*

✧

I believe there are days ahead of returning hope and goodness.

✧

A Coin in a Cup

The famous financier, Baron de Rothschild, once posed for artist Ary Scheffer. The baron dressed himself as a beggar in rags and tatters and held a tin cup to make the point that you can't judge people's value by the way they look.

During the painting session one day, a friend of the artist came into the room, but the baron was so well disguised that the man didn't recognize him. Thinking the baron was really a beggar, the visitor dropped a coin into his cup.

Ten years later the man who gave the coin to Rothschild received a letter containing a bank draft for ten thousand francs and the following message: "You one day gave a coin to Baron de Rothschild in the studio of Ary Scheffer. He has invested it and today sends you the capital which you entrusted to him, together with the compounded interest. A good action always brings good fortune." The note was signed by Baron de Rothschild.

What a concept! If our society could grasp the truth and importance of that statement and put it into practice, this world would be transformed from greedy to generous. People would stop stealing and start giving away their wealth. Businesspeople would look for opportunities to lower their prices instead of raise them. Abuse would come to a screeching halt, and kindness would take its place. Prejudice would become patience. The hungry would be fed, the homeless would be housed, and murder and hatred would be only unpleasant memories.

The power of good in this world is awesome . . . when it's put to work. Good is like a huge reservoir of oil beneath the surface of the earth—rich beyond imagining—and yet, primarily untapped. When ignited, it has phenomenal power, but as long as it lies dormant under the earth, it's useless.

The Price of Fairness

In the early years of wildcat oil drilling, H. L. Hunt was highly successful. In fact, he was often called the richest man in the world. He bought land leases by the thousands in Louisiana, Arkansas, and East Texas, but he paid the landowners a fair price for them. He refused to take financial advantage of other people.

When Mr. Hunt decided to move his family from Tyler to Dallas, he went ahead to look for a home. He found a big house situated on White Rock Lake that was a copy of George Washington's famous Mount Vernon home. The owner was asking sixty-nine thousand dollars for the huge house and all the land surrounding it—a small price for the mansion and property, even in those early days.

The Realtor told Mr. Hunt, "As you can see, it's an expensive house, but it has dirt driveways. Mr. Pickett ran out of money toward the end, and he's had even more severe financial reversals since then. He's asking sixty-nine thousand in cash. However, I know that he would be susceptible to a lower cash offer."

Mr. Hunt said, "Mr. Pickett's figure is acceptable to me."

"You could offer him less. Start at fifty . . ."

Mr. Hunt interrupted, "No, if he's asking sixty-nine thousand, then that's what we'll pay, *especially* if he's desperate."

✧

> Good deeds do not go unrewarded . . . in the long run.

✧

After the papers were signed on the house and the money had been paid, Mr. Pickett told Mr. Hunt how to take care of his best jersey cow and the chickens that went along with the property.

On their way out of the meeting, Mr. Hunt said to his eldest daughter, Margaret, "I didn't mean to take the poor man's cow too."

Was H. L. Hunt a perfect man? By no means, as other parts of his well-known life reveal, but as time went by, he became the richest man in the world—a multibillionaire. And he often used his money to help others, to promote good, and to encourage right. He was willing to pay the price for fairness. Good deeds do not go unrewarded . . . in the long run. He cast his bread upon the waters, and it came back smeared with oil!

A Good Egg

When President Grover Cleveland was a boy, he often found an egg laid on his side of the fence by a neighbor's hen. Now, an egg seems to be no big deal to most of us. And yet, Grover Cleveland, even as a boy, insisted on taking the egg home to the neighbor every time. It was the honest thing to do. It was a good thing to do. It marked Cleveland early in life as an honest and trustworthy person—worthy to become president of the United States someday. His good action resulted in his good fortune—perhaps not immediately, but eventually.

One Step toward Goodness

How do we get started on the return road to goodness? Do we form congressional committees to study the matter? Do we create government agencies to do research and propose public programs for good? Do we have the legislature amend the constitution and revise the laws of the land?

No. We start on a much smaller scale. We start, as the song says, "with the man in the mirror." We begin with one purposeful act of goodness ourselves, by doing one kind thing for one other person. We start by touching one other life with gentleness and care, who in turn will touch another life. We begin by simply lighting a single candle in the darkness, like Mother Teresa, Grover Cleveland, and Immanuel Kant—each just one person doing good.

I am reminded of 1992 when Helen and I took two of our then teenage grandchildren, Amy and Mark Lemley, to the Olympics in Barcelona, Spain. How exciting it was to see the best athletes from many nations compete in gymnastics, diving, water polo, and track and field. Most of all, I was thrilled to see the love and goodwill exhibited between outstanding representatives of many nations. It's a small world after all, and the Olympics are an example of goodwill and hard work.

As we entered the stadium for the closing ceremonies, we were given a packet of items, including a flashlight. After a thrilling program, including the best of Spain in every area, such as music by Placido Domingo, all the lights were extinguished. A hush moved over the vast audience; then a shout of "Ah!" The entire stadium was lighted as thousands of spectators turned on their individual flashlights.

From darkness to light—not because one person flipped a switch on some giant stadium floodlights, but because each of us did our part by turning on our tiny, individual lights. It was a poignant and powerful moment—one I will never forget.

A similar experience often happens at the end of Neil Diamond concerts, when he begins to sing in his gravelly voice, "Turn on your heart lights." And one by one, people in the audience turn on different kinds of small lights—whatever they have with them—flashlights, candles, lighters. By the end of the song, the darkness in the auditorium has been dispelled, and light is glowing warmly everywhere.

Goodness always dispels the darkness in this world. And we can begin the process by simply turning on our heart lights—one at a time— until lights are glowing around the world. The cost? Nothing, except time, concern, and a little effort. It's a free act of love.

Proactive Good

Often, the acts of goodness we see today are *reactions* to something evil. The dastardly act of bombing the Federal Building in Oklahoma City was responded to by firefighters, medical personnel, churches, government agencies, and individuals who rushed to help the wounded and grieving. That's a good and right reaction, but 167 people were already dead and many others wounded.

✧

Goodness
always dispels
the darkness in
this world.

✧

Our natural resources are disappearing at an alarming rate. Environmentalists are responding by encouraging recycling, planting trees, passing laws for emission control and clean air. That's a good reaction, but the land and environment have been tragically scarred . . . beyond complete restoration in some areas.

Teenagers are dying at a staggering rate—from drug addictions, suicides, gang killings, family abuse. Little by little, agencies and lawmakers have begun responding to evil with good—good laws to help protect the teens and others being murdered needlessly. That's excellent, but it's too little and too late for many. Perhaps, it's even too late for someone who was close to you.

The AIDS epidemic is wiping out a huge section of the world population. We have, unfortunately, only begun to see the devastation this evil will cause. After the denial period elapsed, research teams began searching wildly for a cure. Meanwhile, infected people are dying by the thousands as we desperately try to respond to a disease caused by moral decay—the real cause, which is just now beginning to be addressed.

✧

What we really need is more proactive good, as well as reactive good.

✧

What we really need is more *proactive* good, as well as *reactive* good. We need to search for ways to attack every area of life with good, rather than waiting for deterioration to force us into *re*action. We need to encourage right, not just discourage wrong. We need to teach aggressive good, not just defensive good. We need to promote morality, not just pray for a solution to problems that result from immorality. We need to do good ourselves, individually, and help others to do good too.

Only when we become shining stars ourselves will we begin to convert our self-destructive society to a self-preserving society. Only when mothers and fathers become proactive in doing good will families become good places for children to grow up. Only when we allow public-school teachers once again to teach goodness, morality, purity, and right will children learn to be good, moral, pure, and right. Only when we carefully elect good people into government positions will we see consistently good government, good laws, and a good country in which to live.

Ten Ways to Light a Candle in the Darkness

Here are some simple, but effective, ways to be aggressively good and light candles in the darkness around you. Why not choose some of these anybody-can-do-it acts of goodness and put them to work this week?

1. When a merchant gives you too much change, return the overpayment and say, "I wouldn't want to cheat you."

2. When someone charges you too little for something, point out the mistake kindly and pay the full amount you owe.

3. If you take the local newspaper or some good magazines, offer to pass them along to neighbors or friends so they won't have to pay for them.

4. Write a letter of praise for a public servant who does a good job and send it to the president of his or her company or to the appropriate supervisor, sending a copy to the person about whom you're writing.

5. Send one or more cassettes of Christian music to your local jail or prison for the inmates to hear. Who knows what good influence it might have?

6. Donate your used Christian books to your local public library. Most public libraries have no budget to buy Christian books.

7. Set aside your own interests and schedules for a while to listen to a friend and give honest advice when requested.

8. When the opportunity arises, share your faith in God by telling others how the Lord has blessed you in hard times.

9. Always treat others with Christian courtesy. Don't forget to say "thank you," "please," and "I'm sorry."

10. Show patience and good humor in frustrating situations, such as standing in line, waiting at long traffic lights, and waiting in doctors' offices.

This Little Light of Mine

When our children are tiny, we teach them to sing "This little light of mine, I'm gonna let it shine." I often wonder where along the way to adulthood we quit singing that song and holding up our finger-lights. Somewhere on our way to "success," we hid our lights under the bushels of peer pressure, popularity, and fear of rejection.

Solomon the wise said, "The way of the good person is like the light of dawn, growing brighter and brighter until full daylight. But the wicked walk around in the dark; they can't even see what makes them stumble" (Proverbs 4:18–19).

And Paul told the Christians at Rome, "We should stop doing things that belong to darkness and take up the weapons used for fighting in the light" (Romans 13:12).

When we are aggressive in doing good, individually and collectively, our lights will drive the darkness away and, perhaps, "the good old days" will reappear.

John Wesley summed it up nicely with these challenging words:

> Do all the good you can,
> By all the means you can,
> In all the ways you can,
> In all the places you can,
> At all the times you can,
> To all the people you can,
> For as long as ever you can.

And if we do that, life *will* be good . . . not only for us, but for our children, grandchildren, and generations to come. We can unleash the secret weapon to defeat evil—the awesome power of good. Only by lighting candles in the darkness, one by one, can we ever hope to see the bright light of goodness all around us in the future.

CHAPTER TWO

Good Thinking!

secret

No. 2 – Fill your mind with goodness, or it will be filled with evil; think contentment, forgiveness, and optimism.

Ruth Peale

Chairman of the Board,
Peale Center for Christian Living
and Guideposts, Inc.

Life has many facets: physical, mental, and
spiritual. Goodness must penetrate all three.
Your life is great when your thoughts guide
your daily activity with positive goodness
toward outcomes and consequences. Be
positive, joyful, enthusiastic, Spirit-filled.
And be sure to have fun!

The words of a good person are like pure silver,
but an evil person's thoughts are worth very little.

Proverbs 10:20

The Power of Good Thoughts

T he ceiling swirled into view . . . slowly . . . slowly swimming to a blurry stop and turning an antiseptic green. Blinking, I tried to clear my vision and focus on something familiar. Rolling my head to the right, I saw a face . . . a worried face. It was Helen. Thank God, it was Helen.

"Are you all right?" she asked.

"Uh-huh," I moaned. "What happened?"

"You had a terrible accident. You're in the hospital. You're injured, but the doctors say you'll be all right."

Gradually I was beginning to realize what had happened, and the nightmare came charging through my mind like a wild monster on a movie screen. I turned my face to the wall and cried. It was the worst day of my life. I knew I was completely at fault because I had been drinking, but I didn't know how disastrous my mistake had been. I soon found out as I heard the sad news and as I vaguely recalled the events leading up to the tragedy.

The First Tragedy

The first tragedy had struck the night before when one of our young, capable Pepperdine professors had been killed on campus when his motorbike skidded on a wet incline into a concrete light pole. After his day of teaching, he had played handball in Firestone Fieldhouse and was on his way home. His death was a heart-wrenching blow to all of us on campus. I had brought him to Pepperdine and felt that he was a man of dedication and promise.

Helen went to comfort his wife and daughter, and I turned to a crutch I had begun to use often lately. I went to the nearby grocery store and bought a bottle of alcohol. My normal upbeat, optimistic outlook on life had been missing in recent months. I was blaming it on the Valium the doctor had prescribed for my stress, which left me depressed and lethargic. So, I mistakenly decided that "a little wine for my stomach's sake" would be appropriate.

✧

I turned my face to the wall and cried. It was the worst day of my life.

✧

The Second Tragedy

The next morning was spent in my office handling university business. I talked to Malcolm Muggeridge in England, arranging his visit to the campus to lecture in the spring. About eleven o'clock I left for a meeting in Los Angeles with Don Darnell, chairman of our president's board. It was a drive I made most every day, forty-five minutes down Pacific Coast Highway to the freeway and into the heart of the city. I knew I wasn't feeling well, but I thought I could make it, and the meeting wasn't one I could easily postpone or miss.

About five miles from the campus, near the Getty Museum, my vision suddenly blurred badly. I shook my head and blinked my eyes to regain focus, but it just got worse. Then I blacked out completely. My car rammed into the back of a car stopped at the traffic light in front of me. It was a two-door Ford Falcon with a trailer hitch on the rear bumper. When my car hit the Falcon, the trailer hitch was jammed into the Ford's rear gas tank, causing it to explode. Then my car caught fire too.

Two older women—sisters—in the back seat of the Falcon were killed. The driver, who was the daughter of one of the women, was injured. I was also injured.

Fortunately, I was pulled unconscious from my burning car by a man from a nearby home. Then I was transported to the hospital in an ambulance. When I finally regained consciousness, I was in the hospital looking into Helen's face. I had lacerations on my face, a brain concussion, and internal bleeding for several days.

As my mind cleared, my physical injuries were nothing compared to my agony of heart. My sense of guilt was overwhelming. *Why couldn't I have died in the crash?* I thought. *O God, help me! Please help those I have injured. Sustain their crushed families. Forgive me. Help me. Forgive me.*

Questions sliced at me like knives. Would I ever be able to face life again? What would happen to my family? What would happen to the university? I had disgraced them all.

Although I was unaware of it at first, news of the accident was everywhere—in the newspapers, on television, on radio. It was even on Paul Harvey's radio program. The chancellor of Pepperdine University—a Christian university—and a well-known minister for over forty years, was guilty of drunk driving and of killing two people. I was clearly at fault. I could even go to prison for negligent homicide and driving under the influence. Over and over I pleaded, *O God, please help me!*

Compounding the tragedy, news of the accident was disrupting major plans for the university. In two days we were to have the president of the United States, Gerald Ford, on campus to dedicate the

Firestone Fieldhouse and the Brock House, our newly completed president's home. Great effort and expense had gone into preparation. Bleachers were being erected for thousands of expected guests. Security measures were very tight because of a recent attempt on the president's life.

The entire campus community was in a state of incredulous panic. University president, Bill Banowsky, my closest friend and coworker, who was directing the coming celebration, was devastated but determined to do what was best for me and the school. Our constant prayer was that God would show us the way.

Our three daughters and one son-in-law were quickly at my bedside. Our son, Matt, flew home from medical school in Houston. We all prayed together. Close friends, business associates, and coworkers came and prayed. Calls came in from all over the country. Over two thousand telegrams, cards, and letters flooded the Pepperdine offices, our home, and the hospital. Even strangers expressed their concern for us.

Our friend Ralph Sweet from Austin, Texas, flew to Los Angeles immediately to help. Dr. Paul Davis, education editor of the *Reader's Digest*, arrived from San Francisco at the hospital with his suitcase, announcing that he planned to stay and help Helen handle the problems caused by this tragedy. The hospital provided him a room next to mine, and he did just that for days, talking to the press, greeting visitors, and advising Helen.

As I was physically recovering, my thinking was completely confused. Truthfully, some of our family and friends wondered if I might even consider suicide because I was so mentally and emotionally distraught. They were afraid to leave me alone. But they couldn't have been more frightened than I was. Thoughts of what I had done terrified me. My entire life seemed to have crashed and burned in that accident. Life looked bleak and hopeless.

Overcome with shame, I prayed earnestly and continually for God's forgiveness. I read Psalms, especially David's poignant confession of his sins:

God, be merciful to me because you are loving. Because you are always ready to be merciful, wipe out all my wrongs. Wash away all my guilt and make me clean again. I know about my wrongs, and I can't forget my sin. You are the only one I have sinned against; I have done what you say is wrong. . . . Create in me a pure heart, God, and make my spirit right again. Do not send me away from you or take your Holy Spirit away from me. Give me back the joy of your salvation. . . . God, save me from the guilt of murder, God of my salvation, and I will sing about your goodness. (Psalm 51:1–14)

It's impossible to know how many times I read that passage and prayed it as my own desperate prayer. My joy was gone. My thinking was askew. My soul was in agony.

Good Thinking

From a prison cell—a dank, dark, miserable armpit of the Roman Empire—the apostle Paul, faced with rats, disease, aching cold, and torturous death, wrote to his friends who were concerned for him. He didn't write about their physical well being. He didn't express his worry about their finances, their social standings, or even the dangers they faced. Instead, he cautioned them about their thinking and wrote, "Brothers and sisters, think about the things that are good and worthy of praise. Think about the things that are true and honorable and right and pure and beautiful and respected" (Philippians 4:8).

Paul was reminding his friends about a basic and profound principle of mental, emotional, and spiritual health—good thinking. The millions of people filling our psychiatric hospitals and penitentiaries have usually been overwhelmed by thinking about the evils of life. Other millions outside these institutions have minds twisted and hearts darkened by constantly thinking about the world's ugliness and cruelty. They have stopped thinking good thoughts. The candles

27

of their minds have been puffed out by the winds of negative thinking and fear.

What about you? Do you face the future expecting everything to get worse instead of better? Do you fear what will happen for your country and the world? Are you afraid of the future for the church, for your children and grandchildren, and for yourself?

If the answer is yes, I challenge you to consider eight powerful ways to develop and keep good thinking as part of your life.

Eight Facets of Good Thinking

For many of us, *good* thinking must begin with *new* thinking, because our old way of thinking isn't good. Until now, perhaps we have been thinking as the world thinks. Unfortunately, that's just not good thinking. We must think differently from the people around us:

✧

If we don't fill our minds with goodness, they will be filled with evil.

✧

"Do not change yourselves to be like the people of this world, but be changed within by a new way of thinking. Then you will be able to decide what God wants for you; you will know what is good and pleasing to him and what is perfect" (Romans 12:2).

The Bible is plain that our thinking patterns can and, indeed, *must* be changed. We're not stuck with the way we currently think. Paul told the Christians in Philippi this: "In your lives you must think and act like Christ Jesus" (Philippians 2:5). The *must* in this directive suggests that we can choose to have the mind of Christ or we can choose to reject it.

Oliver Barclay once said, "Fundamentally, to love God with all our minds is to let God's revealed truth work through our lives so that our thinking, our attitudes, our worship, and our deeds are consistent. They should all be the result of God's holiness and love and grace toward us. . . . The

28

Bible, when it talks of the mind, is not asking us to develop a (personal) philosophy . . . but to allow revealed truth to control us."

Our minds are not vacuums. They must be filled with something. If we don't fill our minds with goodness, they will be filled with evil.

Here are eight positive ways to ensure that your thinking is good and that the vacuum is filled. Light these eight candles in your life, and you will surely drive the darkness out of your mind and your thinking.

1. THINK SIMPLY

There is a power in the simple life that cannot be found in the cluttered life. A cluttered life usually results in cluttered thinking. And cluttered thinking results in confusion, discontentment, and self-centeredness.

Cluttered thinking may eventually lead to what therapists call Obsessive Compulsive Disorder (OCD). In other words, the more complicated life becomes, the more out of control it will seem, the more we will try to control it, and the more complicated it will become. If the cycle repeats itself at an elevated level because we do not simplify our lives and thinking, the need to control our out-of-control lives becomes even more desperate. It becomes a compulsion, an obsession, and even a disorder.

2. LEARN CONTENTMENT

After her first day in preschool, our little four-year-old granddaughter, Madeline, came home excited.

Madeline's mother said, "How was school, sweetheart?"

Madeline said, "It was wonderful! Everybody likes me." Pause. "The ones who don't like me just don't know me yet."

You see, Madeline is quite content with who she is. She thinks she is wonderful (and we quite agree, of course), so she expects everyone else to think she's wonderful too. And perhaps they will.

29

Contentment is such a valuable possession. And yet, so few of us actually possess it. In my estimation, lack of contentment is one of the greatest caverns in the souls of modern men and women. It is a gaping hole in our society and our personal lives. It haunts us, torments us, and nags at us endlessly. Because we don't have it, contentment is a constant source of irritation and mental chaos. We look for it, we chase it, we long for it. We try to capture it, like a little child who tries to capture a beautiful butterfly and put it in a jar for show-and-tell time at school. We want to own it, but we are rarely able to catch it. Just as we get close to it, contentment flits away from us.

Contentment comes from within, not from without. It may come from being sure, like Madeline, that "everybody likes me." But it certainly comes from knowing that God loves you. We all need to hold on to that basic truth. But how can we grasp it? How can we have that warm inner glow of contentment that comforts us like a potbellied stove on a snowy morning?

Regrettably, I personally believe that our philosophers, therapists, psychiatrists, counselors, and even ministers have unintentionally led us off the mental gangplank to emotional drowning. For decades we've been hearing that, in order to get our thinking straightened out, we need to develop strong self-esteem. They preach that self-worth is our inherent right as a person. They hang all our recovery from depression and hopelessness on feeling good about *self*. And we listen eagerly, hoping for a rescue boat to save us from being mentally adrift in the sea of discontentment and depression.

Meanwhile, every morning we get up and look in our mirrors, fully aware that *self* has a lot of flaws. We're painfully familiar with those flaws and where they came from. We see them plainly, like warts on the face of life that can't be overlooked or forgotten. They can't be hidden with makeup or shaved off with a razor. They are part of who we are and what made us into the people we see in our mirrors today. They are the wrinkles in our faces. They are, in fact, the thoughts that throw our esteem of self into the trash.

So, trying to look at self's hideous flaws while basing our personal worth and contentment on self just doesn't work for most of us. And the word *self-esteem* becomes a hopeless, meaningless, impossible goal, leading us even farther down the road to depression and discontentment.

I can tell you personally that if my mental recovery from the devastation of my accident had been based on esteem of *self*, I would be in a padded room today . . . or worse. Any esteem I had ever had of self was totally destroyed with a mind-shattering crash and its tragic consequences. Self was left in a pile of burning rubble in the middle of that Malibu intersection. It was not something to be esteemed or considered worthy of praise.

✧

When God is allowed to reside within you, personal worth becomes possible.

✧

As well-known writer Eric Hoffer once put it: "The remarkable thing is that we really love our neighbors as ourselves; we do unto others as we do unto ourselves. We hate others when we hate ourselves. We are tolerant toward others when we tolerate ourselves. We forgive others when we forgive ourselves. It is not love but hatred of self which is at the root of the troubles that afflict our world."

Thank God, I found a basis of esteem in me that is flawless, worthy of praise, able to withstand scrutiny, capable of bearing the weight of my worthlessness and still remain a lighted candle in my darkness. God lives in me! My soul is inhabited by the Spirit of my holy and perfect God. And even though self is not worthy of esteem, God within me is worthy to be worshiped, praised, glorified, and magnified. He is why I can look in the mirror without shame and without personal condemnation. He is why I can be content with who I am and know that he is remaking me into his image.

It is when God is allowed to reside within you that personal worth becomes possible. But that worth is based not on *self*-esteem but on *soul*-esteem. As Paul said, "Then you will be innocent and without any wrong. You will be God's children without fault. But you are living with crooked and mean people all around you, among whom you shine like stars in the dark world. You offer the teaching that gives life" (Philippians 2:15–16). You shine like stars in their darkness, lighting the way to hope and life.

Find the elusive contentment you need by seeking the ultimate source of contentment—God himself. Let him fill your life and your-*self;* then your thinking will be anchored in goodness, holiness, and righteousness. You can always ride the storms of life when you're anchored in God.

3. DEVELOP HOPE AND OPTIMISM

During his commencement address to our Pepperdine graduating class in the university's outdoor amphitheater overlooking the blue Pacific, my dear friend, Norman Cousins, made this observation: "No one knows enough to be a pessimist."

Norman, long-time distinguished editor of the *Saturday Review of Literature* and bestselling author, gave hope to countless ill people through his own valiant battle against a dread disease and his refusal to give up in the face of death. He actively fought to live and was very much alive as long as he lived. On this occasion he noted an increasing mood of despair in our world. One of the difficulties with despair is that it leads to helplessness, and helplessness leads to panic, and panic leads to disaster.

Norman was right. No one knows enough about what the future holds to be an informed pessimist. For instance, in the early 1970s, who would have predicted the breakdown of the Berlin Wall or the fall of communism?

One of my favorite quotes is an old Jewish proverb: "If you want to give God a good laugh, tell him your plans." In other words, human beings simply can't see into the future. We can't possibly know if tomorrow's going to be wonderful or worrisome, splendid or splintered, harried or happy. We can only trust God and follow the teaching of Jesus: "Don't be anxious." We must accept each morning as a gift from God. As the old adage says, "Today is a gift; that's why it's called *the present.*" Psalm 118:24 reminds us that "This is the day that the Lord has made. Let us rejoice and be glad today."

Since we can't really know the future, why not be optimistic? Why not hope for the best? Why not think positively? And if we live in hope today, we have a 100 percent chance of making today better than it will be if we live in despair.

Not only do poets, philosophers, and dreamers agree that an optimistic attitude is beneficial to your health, wealth, and well-being, but also doctors, therapists, educators, and lots of other wise people. But is it possible to maintain optimism and hope in a decade when news about the world seems to be more bad than good?

Yes! say those doctors, therapists, educators, and other wise people. They can also explain why some people are almost always cheerful, while others seem to remain in the dumps. Optimism, they say, is a learned condition; there is no such thing as being doomed to unhappiness and gloom.

Here are three effective ways to avoid pessimism and negative thinking:

> ✧
>
> Optimism is a learned condition; there is no such thing as being doomed to unhappiness and gloom.
>
> ✧

Remember that bad things happen to everyone.
Jesus said, "In this world you will have trouble, but be brave! I have defeated the world" (John 16:33). You're not the only one who has problems. Everyone has some kind of problems. Bad things happen in spite of our best efforts to avoid them. That's just how life is. Every person's life is a constant battle of good versus evil. You're not alone.

33

Don't be an alarmist. Just because something bad happens in one area of your life, don't decide that you are under general attack. Leave bad things that happen where they belong—in the past where they happened. Don't bring them into the present or project them into the future. There is power in expectancy. Expect the best, and you're more likely to receive the best.

Know that trouble is often temporary. Even when something bad does happen, as it inevitably will from time to time, don't decide that it will stay that way. Tomorrow may be better. The sun may shine tomorrow, even though it's cloudy today. Rainbows always come after the storm.

Optimists don't always escape pain and suffering. They don't mindlessly say, "Every day in every way I'm getting better and better." A big part of optimism and hope is smiling through the tears.

The writer Václav Havel once spoke of hope in this way:

> I am not an optimist, because I am not sure that everything ends well. Nor am I a pessimist, because I am not sure that everything ends badly. I just carry hope in my heart. Hope is a feeling that life and work have a meaning. You either have it or you don't, regardless of the state of the world that surrounds you.
>
> Life without hope is an empty, boring and useless life. I cannot imagine that I could strive for something if I did not carry hope in me. I am thankful to God for this gift. It is as big a gift as life itself.

Hope is the eager expectation of the good we desire. The Christian's hope is centered in Christ, who overcame death and has already won the victory over evil. He is "the hope of glory" in us that looks forward to his coming again to receive us unto himself.

This basic hope makes us optimistic about life in spite of all that goes wrong. This confidence keeps us going when those without hope give up in despair. It actually provides us with hidden strength to carry on toward our ultimate goal.

But the focus of our hope is not in our own righteousness; it's in the goodness of Christ. To emphasize him is to spread hope, both within and without. Christ said it himself: "Without me they can do nothing" (John 15:5), but "God can do anything" (Luke 1:37).

4. BE ENTHUSIASTIC

Shpilchis is a Yiddish idiom that, when freely translated, means, "I'm so excited I feel like I'm on pins and needles." It's that prickly feeling that skitters up your spine and says, "Let's get moving! I can't wait any longer." *Shpilchis* is a good way to think and a good way to feel about life and living. And it's a lot like the word *enthusiasm.*

Often when we dig into the history of a word, we uncover some surprising facts about its meaning. *Enthusiasm* is just that way. The word comes from the ancient Latins, who combined the word *en* (meaning "in") with *theos* (meaning "god"). In practical usage, the Latins defined an enthusiastic person as one who possesses a god within himself. It's a perfect expression of the essence of a truly enthusiastic person—someone so charged with love and energy that he or she appears to be possessed by a personal god. For Christians, it *is* our personal God. And it's directly connected to soul-esteem.

Enthusiasm is, without a doubt, one of the most important ingredients in a productive and successful life. Enthusiastic people usually have well-developed intellects and seem to react to life with all of their senses charged to the fullest. They not only feel with great passion and intensity, they genuinely care. And they are not ashamed of their enthusiasm, expressing it openly and often.

> ✧
>
> The Latins defined an enthusiastic person as one who possesses a god within himself.
>
> ✧

35

This is why we're so attracted to enthusiastic people. We yearn to share their excitement and love of the world. It's one of the reasons we delight so in the company of children. Since all of life's treasures are new to them, children radiate enthusiasm in its most intense, pure, and innocent form.

Enthusiasm is a necessity for good thinking. Like self-worth, it is based on the recognition of God within you: *en-theos*.

5. CLAIM THE LAW OF APPROPRIATION

The Law of Appropriation says this: As Christians we can claim as our very own the skills, talents, and accomplishments of our brothers and sisters in Christ. When they succeed, we succeed. When they are honored, we are honored. When they are blessed, we are blessed. In this sense we appropriate their achievements as our own.

What a mental high that can be! To think that when Carman sings, it's really me singing. When my friend Joni Eareckson Tada paints, I could sign my name at the bottom. When Max Lucado writes so powerfully about Jesus, I am the coauthor. Or when a fellow Christian is blessed financially, I am richer. Because we are "one in the Spirit," I can appropriate or claim their blessings and talents as my own. I belong to them, and they belong to me. As Paul said to the Corinthian Christians, "If one part of the body suffers, all the other parts suffer with it. Or if one part of our body is honored, all the other parts share its honor" (1 Corinthians 12:26).

Thus, I am thrilled at every accomplishment of good, whether done by me or someone else, because "God alone is good"; so any good thing that is done is a reflection of God, my Father. I no longer have any reason to envy or be jealous of my brothers and sisters, nor they of me. Once this principle is understood and accepted, my sense of achievement is multiplied, and the joy of watching fellow Christians succeed is more exciting day by day.

As a Christian, my family is not limited to brothers and sisters with whom I work and worship regularly. I claim a part of every

Christian in the world—not only the ones living now, but all who have ever lived and even those who are yet to be born. It's no wonder that I'm eager to keep up with the activities of my family around the world. Every good thing they do is mine to enjoy and appropriate into my life.

God intended for this identification of ourselves with the noble accomplishments of others to be a source of satisfaction and strength. The more we grow in Christ, the larger will be our area of appropriation and the keener will be the joy of every day. This joy is a direct result of good thinking on our part—the good thinking that results from appropriation.

6. ADOPT THE ATTITUDE OF GRATITUDE

How long has it been since you said to your employer, "Thank you for a job that gives me a sense of significance and supports my family"?

How long has it been since you told your parents, "Thank you for being who you are and for making me who I am"?

How long has it been since you have expressed appreciation to your teachers, your elders, your children, your employees, and your colleagues for the good influences they have on your life and the lives of your family?

Perhaps you're waiting for them to be perfect. If so, you will wait forever. Perhaps you think that you're mistreated, misunderstood, unloved and, therefore, have no cause for thanksgiving. You're perfectly willing to be most grateful when there is genuine cause for gratitude. In the meantime, you complain, grouse, and criticize those who fail to give you your just due.

> ✧
>
> There is little, if any, correlation between the condition people find themselves in and their ability to be grateful.
>
> ✧

Has it occurred to you that everyone can claim mistreatment, and that if thanksgiving must wait for perfection it will vanish from the earth? The truth is, thankfulness is not necessarily related to your circumstances. The healthiest, wealthiest, and most honored person can feel miserable, ungrateful, and unappreciated. The poorest impoverished inmate can be grateful for the smallest kindness. There is little, if any, correlation between the condition people find themselves in and their ability to be grateful. The question is not one of degree of blessing, but one of attitude. The attitude of gratitude is powerful for happiness. Good attitudes and good thinking go hand in hand.

Matthew Henry, the English author, was once accosted by thieves and robbed of his wallet and money. Still, he could find something to be thankful for. He wrote these words in his diary: "Let me be thankful first, because I was never robbed before; second, because, although they took my purse, they did not take my life; third, because, although they took my all, it was not much; and fourth, because it was I who was robbed, not I who robbed."

In our human predicament, Jesus comes to bring good news—not that we, as people, have solved all our problems, but that God in Christ has made it possible for any one of us, regardless of our race or nationality, to be redeemed. This means joy! This means thanksgiving. This means that we can appreciate even a cup of cold water or a smile or a chance to serve because God is behind all that is good and true and beautiful. This means that our whole attitude is changed from one of hostility and resentment and self-assertion to love and self-expression in thanksgiving.

Christ does not teach us to concentrate on what God owes us, but rather on what we owe God. We need to find the joy of letting go of our uptight self-centeredness and thank both God and people for every opportunity. When you see how much you owe God, you will be thankful for every kindness you receive from others. Gratitude to God is the basis for thankfulness to every human being who touches your life for good.

Dr. Alexander Whyte of Edinburgh, Scotland, was famous for his pulpit prayers. He always found something to thank God for, even in bad times. One stormy morning, a disgruntled member of his congregation thought to himself, *The preacher will have nothing to thank God for on a wretched morning like this.* But Whyte began his prayer, "We thank Thee, O God, that it is not always like this." Surely we, too, can always find a way, even in the worst of times, to thank God for his power, wisdom, goodness, grace, love, care, and mercy.

Good thinking rests firmly on an attitude of gratitude! "Give thanks whatever happens. That is what God wants for you in Christ Jesus" (1 Thessalonians 5:18).

7. MAINTAIN A FORGIVING SPIRIT

A group of Moravian missionaries once decided to take the message of God to the Eskimos. One of their struggles in teaching the Eskimos was that they could not find a word in the Eskimo language for *forgiveness.* Finally, they had to compound a phrase to use in the place of *forgiveness.* This compound phrase turned out to be *issumagijoujungnainermik.* It's a formidable looking assembly of letters, but the expression has a beautiful connotation for those who understand that it means "not being able to think about it anymore."

One of the facets of good thinking is forgiveness. You simply cannot harbor thoughts of hate and anger and be thinking good thoughts at the same time. Forgiveness is a mind-cleansing, thought-cleansing catharsis. It eliminates mental and emotional garbage.

Is there someone in your life that you have refused to forgive? Is your mind wounded with the shrapnel of an exploded relationship? Do you retain hatred, resentment, and anger toward someone you feel has wronged you? If so, who is in pain?

We often mistakenly believe that holding back forgiveness inflicts some kind of damage on our enemy. Not so! Our own minds and thinking are damaged by our refusal to forgive. The wounds remain festered in our own hearts and minds until the salve of forgiveness is generously applied. Only then can good thinking, productivity, and happiness return in full measure.

Leonardo da Vinci was one of the outstanding geniuses of all history, for he was great as a draftsman, an engineer, a thinker, and an artist. Just before he began his work on his painting the "Last Supper," he had a violent quarrel with a fellow painter. Leonardo was so angry that he decided to paint the face of his enemy, the other artist, into the face of Judas, and thus take his revenge by picturing the man in infamy to succeeding generations. The face of Judas was, then, one of the first that he finished, and everyone could easily recognize it as the face of the painter with whom da Vinci had quarreled.

But when Leonardo came to paint the face of Christ, he could not go on. Something seemed to be holding him back, baffling him, and frustrating his best efforts. At length he came to the conclusion that the thing which was checking his progress was his enemy's face painted on Judas. So he painted out the face of Judas and began anew on the face of Jesus, this time with the success that has been acclaimed down through the ages.

You cannot at one and the same time be painting the features of Christ into your own life and painting another face with the colors of evil and hatred. Only forgiveness allows the true features of Christ to come through in your own thinking and life. Without forgiveness good thinking is impossible.

Self-forgiveness, as I came to find out after my accident, is the first place to begin in restoring good thinking. Life simply slams to a stop emotionally and mentally when self-incrimination overrides God's grace and forgiveness.

I won't tell you that I regained my optimism and hope quickly after my accident, because I didn't. The monstrous nightmare often roared through my mind and left me in devastation and depression all over again. It was a slow crawl, one painful day at a time, back to healing.

And I won't tell you that good thinking eliminates the consequences of previous bad thinking. I still had to face the legal consequences of my actions. It was a long and excruciating process, but slowly it came to a resolution. The university was very considerate in putting me on leave until the court case was concluded. An excellent attorney, whom Bill Banowsky helped me select, developed a proposed plan of punishment for me, which involved, among other things, a long-term research project at the Safety Center at the University of Southern California.

Business friends supported this project financially. Out of this research came a book titled *Poison Stress Is a Killer* based on statistical data related to the effects of stress in drunk-driving cases. The judge accepted this research as partial punishment. In addition, I served several years of a probated sentence and spent thousands of hours in community service.

By this time I realized that I could be helpful to others who were victims of alcoholism. I made hundreds of talks across the country to schools, churches, and civic groups. I tried to be as forthright as possible in confessing my guilt.

I had spent the first fifty years of my life not touching alcohol. In fact, I had often lectured against it. Now, from personal and painful experience, I spoke of the need for abstinence and the dangers of alcohol as I shared my story.

The Pepperdine trustees, under Tom Bost's leadership, were forbearing and supportive. Bill Banowsky and Charles Runnels were extremely helpful. I was reinstated as chancellor and served the university another ten years in that role and, now, have served more than ten years as chancellor emeritus. I vowed that, if I could get that experience behind me, I would work harder than ever to justify their confidence.

Gradually, I began to accept personally something else I had preached for forty years. I realized that God loved me in spite of all that had happened, in spite of all my failures, in spite of all my sins, and that he had forgiven me because Christ paid the price for my sins, not because I am good.

I also learned much about the goodness of people during this tragedy. Some said, "The world will forgive you, but the church will not." But this has *not* been true. Of the two thousand letters and telegrams we received, all but four were full of love, forgiveness, and support. I had many donations to help with the legal costs. People I barely knew, and some I didn't know at all, sprang to my assistance. I owe them all an undying debt of gratitude.

I was also publicly forgiven by the gracious woman who was driving the car I hit and whose mother was killed. When the press asked her about how she thought her mother would feel about me, she replied that her mother would have been the first one to offer Christian charity and forgiveness. Then she said that she had forgiven me too. I will ever be grateful to her and her family.

✧

Good thinking is a habit that can be developed.

✧

My gratitude goes most of all to God, who loves me, forgave me, sustained me, comforted me, and gave me a new heart and a new mind. My thinking was renewed and refreshed through him. My joy and hope returned because of him. My life became worth living again because of him.

I learned the truth of what Peter Marshall said: "It is in times of calamity . . . in days and nights of sorrow and trouble, that the presence, the sufficiency, and the sympathy of God grows very sure and wonderful. Then we find out that the grace of God is sufficient for all our needs, for every problem, for every difficulty, for every broken heart, and for every human sorrow."

In a sense, there are no real tragedies for the Christian. There are lessons to learn from difficulties that make the saddest situation a blessing. Thank God for the trials of life.

8. ACCENTUATE THE POSITIVE

Good thinking is a habit that can be developed. It's not an elusive mental power that only a few superbrains can master. True, it doesn't come without effort, but the effort is definitely worthwhile.

I'm a living, breathing, joyful testimony to that. Only when I began to refocus my thinking on God and away from myself—back on the source of all good—did my healing really begin.

Here are some practical, workable things I learned along the way, as the old song says, to "accentuate the positive and eliminate the negative" in my thinking. Perhaps they will be of some help to you too. Do these consistently, along with the eight suggestions made in this chapter, and you'll be amazed at the positive changes God will make in your life.

1. Always visualize yourself as victorious, with God's help. "In all these things we have full victory through God who showed his love for us" (Romans 8:37).

2. Cancel negative thoughts with faith thoughts. "Be joyful because you have hope. Be patient when trouble comes, and pray at all times" (Romans 12:12).

3. Believe in yourself because God believes in you. "Remember those days in the past when you first learned the truth. You had a hard struggle with many sufferings, but you continued strong. . . . So do not lose the courage you had in the past, which has a great reward" (Hebrews 10:32, 35).

4. Mentally minimize problems and maximize God's power. "But the Lord is faithful and will give you strength and protect you from the Evil One" (2 Thessalonians 3:3).

5. Keep an open mind. Always learn, grow, and improve yourself. "We will grow up in every way into Christ" (Ephesians 4:15).

6. Practice personal affirmations. "I can do all things through Christ, because he gives me strength" (Philippians 4:13).

7. Put your life in God's hands and praise him for your victories. "Trust the Lord with all your heart, and don't depend on your own understanding" (Proverbs 3:5).

CHAPTER THREE

It's a Great Day to Be Alive!

secret

No. 3 – Actively pursue good health by developing good habits for work, sleep, eating, exercise, and positive thinking.

Joni Eareckson Tada

Joni and Friends, Inc.

Considering others is not the art of doing something extraordinary. It is the art of doing a common thing extraordinarily well.

The most trivial action, the slightest smile, the briefest greeting may be considered a service not only to others but to God.

Wise people's lives get better and better.
They avoid whatever would cause their death.

Proverbs 15:24

The Power of Good Health and Habits

As the misty fog lifts over Malibu and the red rays of morning leave a shimmering trail across the quiet Pacific, Helen and I are walking our laps around the track at Pepperdine as we do most every morning. It's our routine, our determined daily workout, our pleasure.

At eighty-one, what am I doing on the track? Am I trying to recapture my youth like Ponce de León? or keep up with Jack LaLaine, who pulled seventy small boats by a rope in his teeth while swimming around the bay on his seventieth birthday? No. It's simple. I'm just trying to make sure I get to eighty-two! And I know that being good to my body is one of the primary keys to making it.

Even when we're traveling, Helen and I take our walking shoes with us and search out a place where we can continue our ritual of good health—in an airport, at the health club in the hotel, or on a city street. We believe in it, we encourage it in others, and we try to consistently practice what we preach.

The Treasure of Good Health

The treasure of good health cannot be overvalued. Most of us would trade all the money and possessions we have, no matter how great, for that glorious feeling of health and vigor. I should know. After chapter 2 of this book was completed and before chapter 3 was begun, I had a mild stroke; this chapter was written while I went through intensive physical therapy in the hospital. Thank God, I'm back to good health now.

As soon as the doctor released me, I went right back to walking at the track. Like the pearl of great price, the treasure of good health is just too valuable to lay aside or treat with apathy. We may have to give up other things, such as time or money, that are important to us in order to obtain and keep the treasure of good health. We all know people who are ill or invalids who would advise us to treasure our health.

Joni Eareckson Tada lives not far from me, and I count it a privilege to know her. One day at breakfast, Joni told me her story.

On a hot July afternoon in 1967, Joni and her sister Kathy went to a beach on the Chesapeake Bay for a swim. The water was dark and murky, and Joni didn't bother to check its depth when she climbed onto a raft anchored offshore.

Joni says, "I positioned my feet on the edge, took a deep breath, and plunged into the water. Sprong! My head hit something hard and snapped back. I felt a strange electric shock in the back of my neck. Under water and dazed, I felt myself floating, drifting, unable to surface.

"My lungs were screaming for air, but just as I opened my mouth to 'breathe' water, I felt my sister's arms around me, lifting me to fresh air.

" 'Kathy,' I spluttered when I saw my lifeless arm slung over her shoulder, 'I can't feel!' "

Joni had broken her neck, and her vibrant, athletic life was abruptly interrupted. She was suddenly paralyzed from her shoulders down. Good health was snatched away.

Joni told me that she went through a bitter time of asking God, "How could you have allowed this to happen to me?" as she faced the prospect of living her life as a quadriplegic. I can understand why she would, can't you? She came to breakfast in her wheelchair. A friend had to feed her. But after a few minutes, as our conversation moved to spiritual things, I was no longer aware of her disability. Vibrance and life shimmered in her eyes, and joy radiated through her conversation.

It certainly would have been easy for Joni to retreat into the darkness of physical pain and limitation. She could have chosen to withdraw from life and become a homebound recluse, nursing her shattered ego and feeling sorry for herself. After all, she'd taken a critical blow to quality of life and, seemingly, had every right to be bitter. And for a few months she was. But her friends were praying for her around the clock. Her strong reliance on God, combined with the application of prayer, changed her life.

Then Joni went to battle for herself. She began applying active good in other ways to her condition. One painful and tedious day at a time, Joni worked with occupational therapists to regain what modicum of muscle activity and control she could over her frozen limbs. She did prayer battles with God and, after finally surrendering her will to his, she came out victorious. Although not healed physically, she is whole and strong spiritually and mentally.

Since then, Joni has written a shelf full of marvelous, best-selling books that encourage others to apply active good to their lives as she does. She paints pictures that glorify God, but she does it the hard way—by holding the brush in her teeth. She sings his praises melodiously. She conducts powerful spiritual seminars and workshops. And she produces educational training materials and programs to help businesses, churches, and service organizations become aware and meet the needs of disabled people. With good thinking, Joni strongly proclaims, "My wheelchair is the prison God has used to set my Spirit free!" She also shares a wonderful marriage with her husband, Ken.

Joni shines like a star everywhere she goes. You can't be around her for long before the light of God shines through her into your life. Her faith and courage inspire millions who read her books, see her paintings, or hear her speak. Joni converted brokenness into blessings, both for herself and for everyone around her. Now, more than twenty-five years later, there is no darkness around Joni Tada. She says she has found the truth of Romans 8:28: "We know that in everything God works for the good of those who love him."

Many of us today are less than healthy *by choice.* We often choose unhealthy lifestyles. We go without proper rest; we work too many hours; we drink too much caffeine; we eat fats instead of leans; we watch television instead of going for walks or working out; we don't go in for regular checkups; we smoke or drink or put other dangerous and/or addictive *stuff* in our bodies.

❖

"My wheel-
chair is the
prison God
has used to set
my spirit free!"

❖

Granted, we don't make a once-for-all-time choice to be unhealthy. None of us would purposely do that. Rather, we make the choice one meal at a time, one drink at a time, one couch-potato day at a time. And in ten years we look back and think, *How'd I ever get in this terrible condition?* Or we look in the mirror and say to ourselves, *I've got to go on a diet.*

Good health is, to a large degree, a series of good choices linked together for a lifetime. Every wise choice we make, no matter how small, is a choice for good health; every unwise choice we make, no matter how small, is a choice for poor health. We may not see the results of those small choices immediately, but we can be certain that we'll see them eventually.

From Death to Life

In 1982 I wrote an endorsement for a small booklet titled *One of the Survivors* and written by Richard Taylor. Richard was shot nine times in the back and chest by a "friend" and left for dead on the side of an Oklahoma highway. By some miracle he survived. When he was well enough, he was transferred to prison where he expected to spend the rest of his life. If he had been convicted of all the charges he faced, he could have been sentenced to over five hundred years in prison.

From his prison cell, Richard told his story of how a series of unwise choices had led him from being a happily married premed university student on a full basketball scholarship to using recreational drugs, to moving up to hard drugs, to becoming a pusher, to divorce and committing small crimes, then large crimes, and finally to being shot and left for dead by one of his crime buddies.

While lying in the intensive care unit after surgery, Richard met a minister named Bill Banks, who said that when he entered Richard's hospital room, which was under guard by the sheriff's office and the Oklahoma Bureau of Investigation, "I looked at him, seeing a young man who needed a friend before he died."

Through Bible study with Bill over the next few months, Richard found God, and his life did an about-face. He became a Christian. Soon Richard found out that God had plans for him that no one could have imagined possible. And he began to apply the amazing salve of goodness to his wounded and broken life. The results are astounding!

At Richard's trial, a hard-nosed assistant district attorney was so deeply moved by the amazing support, prayers, and help given to Richard by his new Christian friends that he actually recommended Richard's release. On top of that, a skeptical old judge went completely against his own judicial instincts and granted the release. He dismissed five felony indictments, reduced two others to first-offender status, and sentenced Richard to two concurrent ten-year probations in Oklahoma.

Another judge accepted guilty pleas on thirty-nine misdemeanor charges and sentenced Richard only to the time he had already served in the county jail.

Three years later, the two probations were also dismissed. The convictions were completely set aside based on recommendations of Oklahoma probation officials who had watched Richard doing good. The whole thing was strictly incomprehensible! Only God could have made it happen.

> Good health is a series of good choices linked together for a lifetime.

During those three years following his trial, Richard Taylor spent his life in service to the God who had rescued him. He actively applied goodness and righteousness to his life. Richard limped (a result of the gunshot wounds) onto stages of colleges, high schools, junior high schools, civic clubs, and Sunday schools across the country to tell his incredible story to teens and young adults so they would not make the same unwise choices he had made. His life burned like a brilliant candle in the darkness.

Richard's influence for good is still being felt in the lives of people who avoided drugs or gave up drugs and crime after hearing him speak or talking with him privately. His family, instead of having to live with the shame of a criminal, is living with the confidence and joy of a redeemed Christian.

Like Joni Tada, Richard never again had good physical health. He had given it up one unwise choice at a time in his earlier life. His abused and neglected body—the real victim of his wild living—simply couldn't repair the damage done or go on after a while. Even though his healthy, robust spirit flew into the arms of God, Richard's body died in Fort Worth, Texas, at a premature age, leaving his wife, three children, and thousands of friends and admirers grieving his loss. And yet, he met his Maker spiritually strong and pure as a result of his having applied the power of divine goodness to his once-evil life.

Getting Your Health on Track

If Richard had it to do over again, would he make wiser choices about his life and health? If he could speak to us now, I'm sure that he would offer us urgent advice about holding on to the treasure of good health. In his absence, I'd like to offer some suggestions that can keep us on the right road to physical and mental well-being and stamina.

ASK GOD TO BLESS YOU

God is the giver of life and health. He alone can give health. He alone can repair physical bodies. So the best place to begin your good health program is by asking him to bless you with good health.

In a recent conversation with George Gallup, the well-known pollster, he said that one of the most encouraging tidal waves and best-kept secrets in America is the revolution that's coming through Alcoholics Anonymous and other focus groups who now recognize that we simply cannot cope with illnesses, diseases, and addictions without the help of a higher power.

Take a close look at how some of the people in the Bible appealed to God for good health and the resulting blessings.

- Hannah prayed for God to give her a healthy son, and he did.

- God healed Job's body when the time of testing was over.

- A blind man pleaded for Jesus to open his eyes, and suddenly he could see.

- Ten men with leprosy were given back their good health by God through his Son.

- A crippled man begged Peter and John to help him at the Beautiful Gate, and by the power of Jesus Christ, he was able to walk . . . for the first time in forty years!

- In the desert, God healed all the people of snakebite poisoning who looked to him for healing.

And the stories go on and on through the Bible. God's people of faith have always understood that good health is God's department—it's a precious gift from him.

A 1996 research report from the American Medical Association shows how much difference prayer makes in a person's health. Research was done on a large group of people who had heart-bypass surgery. The results showed that the patients who *prayed for recovery* had a 50 percent higher recovery rate than the ones who didn't pray.

It reminds me of the little girl who was about to have an operation. The surgeon explained that before he could make her well, he would have to put her to sleep.

"All right," said the little girl, "but first I have to say my prayers." Then she kneeled down by the operating table and said, "Now I lay me down to sleep; I pray the Lord my soul to keep. If I should die before I wake, I pray the Lord my soul to take." Then she smiled at the doctor with confidence and climbed up on the table.

All went well with the surgery, and that night the surgeon got down on his knees and prayed for the first time in thirty-five years.

When was the last time you got down on your knees and earnestly prayed for good health? Tonight might be a good time to start. Apply the power of prayer to your health as a *preventative* measure, not just as a repair method.

✧

Good health is God's department— it's a precious gift from him.

✧

INCREASE YOUR BRAIN POWER

The brain is capable of outstanding feats of computation and information processing. Yet, most people use no more than 4 to 10 percent of their brainpower.

According to Richard Leviton, author of *Brain Builders! A Lifelong Guide to Sharper Thinking, Better Memory, and an Age-Proof Mind*, we can increase our brainpower dramatically by using and nourishing it on a consistent basis. He says, "Increasing your brainpower involves exercising and toning your mind." In other words, we have to apply good health habits to our brains too.

Here are five ways Leviton says we should keep our brains healthy and fit:

- Keep our verbal fluency and level of reading comprehension high.
- Keep our mental interests keen and well-practiced.
- Keep our mental attitudes flexible, open, and ready for challenges.
- Keep learning new things, visiting new places, and entertaining new ideas.
- Associate with people who practice these same fundamentals.

Leviton goes on to say, "Brainpower is not separate from who you are and how you live. The state of your body influences the workings of your mind." They go hand in glove. A healthy body helps the mind work better, and a healthy mind (or attitude) helps the body work better. Generally, you don't have one without the other.

PROTECT YOUR MENTAL HEALTH

What is mental health? Is it total happiness? Is it lack of stress? How can it be defined? Perhaps these five characteristics from the Hogg Foundation for Mental Health at the University of Texas can help us understand it better:

1. **Balance.** We need to maintain our equilibrium, recognizing that both pleasure and pain thread our lives. When one is visible in our lives, the other is waiting in the shadows.

2. **Acceptance.** Many people grow indignant over personal difficulties, wasting emotional energy railing at futile situations. Learning to accept what cannot be changed helps us to achieve positive outlooks on life.

3. **Endurance.** "This too shall pass." Those words stand us in good stead in situations that call for forbearance and patience.

4. **Recognition.** Knowing what matters, recognizing the important aspects of life and being willing to let slide those which are not vital can go a long way toward helping us maintain an upbeat approach.

5. **Delight.** It's important to maintain the ability to laugh, to see humor even in tough situations. When we can find delight in everyday happenings, we will lighten our lives overall.

Bless Your Body with Sleep

America has drifted into being a nation of chronically sleep-deprived people. Compared to 1910, the average day of work is four hours longer, and our sleep pattern is two hours shorter. The Better Sleep Council reports that over the past twenty years, Americans have added around 158 hours (or nearly an entire month each year) to our job schedules. That doesn't include the hours we put in working to care for our families and homes. And yet, the Bible says this: "It is no use for you to get up early and stay up late, working for a living. The Lord gives sleep to those he loves" (Psalm 127:2).

Sleep deprivation is caused by both lack of time spent sleeping and poor-quality sleep. According to the AAA Foundation for Traffic Safety, sleep-deprived drivers are vulnerable to micronaps lasting four or five seconds. At highway speeds, that's plenty of time for a fatal crash to occur, as police accident reports will verify. Have you ever caught yourself nodding off at the wheel? I believe sleep deprivation is responsible for far more accidents than the statistics even indicate.

Disrupted sleep and sleep disorders cost American businesses billions of dollars annually in lost productivity, industrial accidents, and higher medical bills, according to government and industry reports.

Dr. David Redman of Johns Hopkins University Medical Center has been studying sleep deprivation in relationship to critical jobs. His research shows, for instance, that lack of sleep was implicated in the Exxon Valdez oil spill. The third-mate pilot had not slept for forty-eight hours when the accident occurred. The space shuttle Challenger disaster is also partially attributed to sleep deprivation, as was the nuclear accident at Three Mile Island.

Dr. Greg Belenky of Walter Reed Army Medical Center tells us that loss of sleep during the night is responsible for increased vulnerability to illness, such as increased cardiovascular risk factors and increased gastrointestinal problems. He says that sleep allows the brain to shut down one section at a time to refurbish itself. Sleep is the brain's repair shop. If that sleep is denied, we have a tendency to nod off at work the next day and suffer a loss of creativity and clarity of thinking. Power tools or heavy equipment can become dangerous weapons in the hands of sleepy operators. And almost everyone is familiar with the physical aches and pains that occur because of poor-quality sleep.

✧

"It is no use for you to get up early and stay up late, working for a living. The Lord gives sleep to thoses he loves."

✧

Dr. Michael Guillen, science editor for *Good Morning, America,* in a 1997 report on the effects of sleep deprivation, said that our body clocks are completely out of sync with the pattern of the sun, which is a frustration to the body. This can be greatly attributed to electric lights and the artificial extension of daylight hours. He calls us the "waking wounded."

Jesus, too, recognized the need for rest. He would, from time to time, escape his hordes of followers to sleep. His physical body demanded it. His stamina required it. His wisdom could not deny it. Bodies must rest or collapse. And bodies that are deprived of sufficient rest on a regular basis are susceptible to all kinds of illnesses, failures, and breakdowns. Sleep is inevitable. It's necessary. It's even enjoyable. Sleep is a beautiful gift from God: "Come to me, all of you who are tired . . . I will give you rest" (Matthew 11:28).

In truth, if we refuse to apply God's good gift of sleep, we're saying that we know more about our bodies than the God who created them. We're flying in the face of wisdom and reality. And we'll likely crash land. Good health and proper rest are inseparable. God didn't give the Sabbath as a joke; he gave it for the rest he knew we would require. Rest is a part of the "happy quotient." My friend, Jeff Walling, puts it so well: "My idea of happy hour is a nap."

LAUGH YOUR WAY TO THE GOOD LIFE

Your good health is affected by your attitude toward life. My friend Norman Cousins proved it. When he was attacked by a terminal illness, he didn't just lay down and die. Norman immediately began counterattacking his disease with good ideas and remedies. One of his most successful attacks was with laughter.

While in the hospital, Norman rented dozens of videos of funny old movies and television series, like *I Love Lucy, The Dick Van Dyke Show, The Carol Burnett Show,* and others. And believe it or not, he literally laughed himself back to better health. I watched him do it.

The medical community confirms that laughter is a healant. By laughing we release certain endorphins into the system that attack disease and general poor health. Laughter relieves stress and pain. It lightens the emotional load of physical illness and disease. Can we explain exactly how it works? No. But does it actually work? Yes!

Psychologists and medical doctors all agree. Even dentists give their patients *laughing gas* to deaden the pain. The Great Physician also agrees: "A happy heart is like good medicine, but a broken spirit drains your strength" (Proverbs 17:22). When the brain sends messages of defeat and gloom through the body, the flow of vitality and energy is blocked. You'll be amazed how much better you'll feel when you practice cheerfulness and just have a good laugh from time to time.

Suppose, though, for a minute that the dissenters are right. Suppose that laughter doesn't actually have any healing power. What have I lost by laughing anyway? I've lost a bit of misery, some unhappiness, and a little depression. I've lost some worry, pessimism, and frustration . . . at least for a few moments. In my opinion, if no other benefits are ever seen, even a few moments of joy and release from negative thinking have to be good for you.

I'll take my chances with laughter. At least someday I'll pass from this life to the next with a smile on my face instead of a scowl.

> ✧
>
> "A happy heart is like good medicine, but a broken spirit drains your strength."
>
> ✧

GET REGULAR CHECKUPS

Mary Mallon worked as a cook for various wealthy families in New York City. Not until 1907, six years after her first job, did disease sleuths from the New York City Department of Health trace her movements from one typhoid-stricken home to another. The newspapers announced that Typhoid Mary was a walking container of deadly typhoid.

The woman was confined and treated for three years. Then she signed a pledge not to work as a cook again, to watch her hygiene, and to report to the Department of Health every three months.

Mary, however, vanished for five years. In 1915 typhoid struck several members of the kitchen staff in a New York hospital. A check of the employees turned up Typhoid Mary. This time, she was put in an institution and remained there until her death in 1938.

Mary wasn't sick herself; she was only a *carrier* of the typhoid disease. We see the same phenomena today with people who are carriers of highly contagious diseases like hepatitis and AIDS. Most times you simply can't tell by looking at these people that they are carrying a deadly disease. And it's the deceptiveness of these attackers that make regular checkups imperative for the rest of us.

In a July 3, 1995, article titled "The Current Situation of HIV/AIDS Pandemic," The American Association for World Health estimated that 19,500,000 people had already been infected with AIDS. They predict that more than 30 to 40 million people will be HIV-positive by the year 2,000.

I'm pleased to see so many doctors, health organizations, and medical associations finally taking a stand against "safe sex" and in favor of *abstention* as the only real prevention to AIDS. The Bible makes it clear that abstention is where God has drawn his line in the sand about extramarital sex. In our world today, good health is on one side of the line, and death may very well be on the other. When we follow his commandments and apply the good of his Word to our lives, we'll find health and happiness. If we choose to ignore his warnings and step over the line, we are likely to find disease and disaster.

Early detection of some diseases allows treatment and cure. And early detection can only come with regular checkups and good health habits. The naive attitude that *it can't happen to me* is pure folly.

✧

The Bible makes it clear that abstention is where God has drawn his line in the sand about extramarital sex.

✧

By actively pursuing good health, we can prevent many disasters from ever happening, rather than waiting for our health to fail and then trying to restore it with reactive good.

My doctor tells me that the reason my stroke was relatively mild was because of our regular regimen of exercise, healthy eating, and other consistent good health habits. I'm a believer, now more than ever! What about you? What good health habits are you actively pursuing to prevent illness?

KICK THE HABIT!

Warning: The Surgeon General Has Determined That Cigarette Smoking Is Dangerous to Your Health. In spite of that official warning, about 50 million people in the United States currently smoke a total of 570 billion cigarettes each year (U.S. Bureau of Statistics).

Laboratory and clinical research have proven conclusively that smoking greatly increases a smoker's risk of dying from several diseases, chief of which is lung cancer. Additionally, smokers have a fivefold increased risk for cancer of the larynx, oral cavity, and esophagus; about one-third of all cancers of the bladder, kidney, and pancreas are attributable to smoking as well. Millions of people still smoke.

Cigarette advertising has been banned from radio and television, cities and states are rapidly passing laws requiring nonsmoking sections in public places and workplaces. And federal law now bans smoking on all domestic airline flights. Still, people smoke.

After the initial warning was put on cigarette packages, over 30 million Americans stopped smoking. They made a choice for good health. And yet, 50 million more people chose to continue smoking, in spite of the proven detriment to their health. They made a choice for bad health.

This same scenario could be painted for a variety of bad habits: alcohol, drugs, eating fat-loaded foods, bulimia, anorexia, and many others. In most cases, the bad habit begins with a single bad choice. And in most cases, the bad habit is perpetuated or stopped by a single choice. Granted, that same choice may have to be made repeatedly in order to stop a bad habit, but each time it's a single choice to apply good, rather than bad, to your health.

Is quitting a bad habit easy? No, it's one of the toughest challenges a person can face. I know, because I had to make that decision for good over and over again after my accident. And over and over again I asked myself, *Why did I ever take that first drink anyway?*

The best and easiest way to stop a bad habit is never to start it. Take an aggressive stand for good against the constant offerings of evil that our culture holds out to you. Simply refuse. Say no. Walk away. Run if you have to! Even if they call you a coward, even if the one offering is your boss or a friend, even if you'll be a society reject—don't do it! It's not worth it . . . no matter what benefits it supposedly offers.

> ✧
>
> Even if they call you a coward, even if you'll be a society reject —don't do it!
>
> ✧

If you've developed a bad habit, and you can't seem to make the choice for good consistently by yourself, get help. Don't wait until you no longer have a choice or until disaster has struck. Do it now! Join a support group. See a counselor. Ask a Christian friend to pray with you. Whatever you need, do it. Don't be embarrassed. You need never be embarrassed to seek help in turning some part of your life from bad to good. It takes enormous courage and great spiritual maturity to choose goodness over evil. And when you've made the choice for good, your victory will be a symbol of hope for others who are struggling with some choice in life as difficult for them as yours is for you.

Each time you avoid a bad habit, you shine like a star. Each time you end a bad habit, you are a living light. And each time you shine, you light the path for others to follow you toward good health.

WHISTLE WHILE YOU WORK

Work is health-giving. To do nothing is to begin to die. Work is energizing, challenging, and occupying. Work is good. And some kinds of work are better than others.

I like the philosophy of the book *Do What You Love, and the Money Will Follow* by J. Sinetar. I find it to be the truth. Working just for work's sake is boring. And working just for the money is unfulfilling. But working for the joy of it, working at something you love, is a dynamic and exciting adventure.

In my opinion, the most fortunate people in the world are the ones who get paid to do what they love to do. They are truly making a living and living life at the same time. Too many people feel that their lives are put on hold while they are at work. They dislike their jobs, are bored with their assigned tasks, and hate getting out of bed in the morning. What a waste! And often it's all in the name of money.

The most successful working people I know love their work. They look forward to going to their offices or jobs and derive great pleasure from the work they do. Why? Because they've found, not just a job, but their life's work, their niche in life, what they are meant to do.

Most often, what people are *meant* to do is what they are *gifted* to do; what they're *gifted* to do, they're *good* at doing; and because they're good at what they do, they usually *succeed.* So those people are often willing to work harder and longer than other employees, not because they are required to, but because they enjoy it.

These people sometimes are ridiculed by the rest of us, though. We mislabel these gifted and happy workers as *workaholics.* Because we see them work long hours and because we're *not* thrilled with the work we're doing, we falsely conclude that they must be *driven* people, that their Puritan work ethic won't allow them to rest or stop to enjoy recreation. The truth is, they're having fun working. Their work *is* their recreation. It's their joy and delight. They're not *driven* to work; they are *called* to work.

Our good friend, Paula Stiger, is a good example. She's a gifted interior arranger/decorator who owns a company called RoomOvers in Fort Worth, Texas. When Paula gets involved in rearranging furniture, rehanging pictures, or making gorgeous floral arrangements out of the weeds in your yard, she just can't quit. Her eyes sparkle when she talks about the vision she can see for a room that she's reworking, and you can just see the wheels in her mind whirling. She sings while she works and she laughs while she works. Oh, she gets tired like the rest of us—but it's a happy tired.

Paula came to our home and helped Helen rearrange our downstairs area. I was amazed at how much work they got done and how much fun they had doing it together. And the minute they finished one room, Paula would say, "Okay, what's next?" She couldn't wait to transform yet another room. Her gift and her work are perfectly matched.

But Paula's teenage daughter, Lauren, thinks Paula's a workaholic. She says her mom never stops working, even when she's at home. True enough. Paula's always rearranging her own furniture, recovering a chair, or moving a painting to keep things fresh at home. But how do you keep a Martha Stewart from making things around her beautiful? It's like asking a fire not to burn or a butterfly not to fly. When you stop them from doing what they're meant to do, they die.

When we focus our work on something positive, helpful, and good, we'll find inner satisfaction and contentment. Work that contributes to the good of people, either directly or indirectly, is good work. Work that glorifies God in one way or another is good work. Work that is honest and respectable, whether it's white-collar, blue-collar, or no-collar, is good work. And people who are busy doing good work rarely have time to do evil things at the same time.

Work is mentally, physically, spiritually, and socially healthful. The important task is to find the work you love, then you can love the work you do. Until you find that special job, though, the Bible tells us how to make the most of the jobs we have: "In all the work you are doing, work the best you can. Work as if you were doing it for the Lord, not for people. Remember that you will receive your reward from the Lord, which he promised to his people. You are serving the Lord Christ" (Colossians 3:23–24). And anytime you're working for Christ, it's good work.

The Five Ps of Good Health

God will always reward us with what we ask of him. If we ask for good health by applying good habits to our lifestyles, he will reward us with good health. If, by our apathy and lack of effort in maintaining our physical strength and vigor, we ask for poor health, we will be rewarded with poor health. Talking to God about good health but never getting out of our chairs to exercise won't do it. We have to match our prayer with our care.

Be proactive with your health! Be demanding with yourself. And don't accept your own excuses. Here are Five Ps for good health:

1. **Push yourself.** Push away from the table. Push away bad habits. And do push-ups to avoid pushing up daisies too soon.

2. **Pull yourself.** Pull yourself out of your chair and down to the gym. Pull yourself up to a salad instead of a steak. Pull out all the stops in preventive medicine.

3. **Promote yourself.** Promote yourself from couch potato to walking wonder. Promote yourself from junk-food junkie to health-food hero. Promote yourself from poor health to good health.

4. **Purify yourself.** Purify your body by eliminating unhealthy foods and drinking lots of water. Purify your daily routine by adding some form of exercise. Purify your Christian image by trimming up and slimming down.

5. **Pray for yourself.** Pray that God will help you take better care of your body. Pray that God will bless you with good health. Pray that God will give you the courage and determination to follow his Word: "You should know that your body is a temple for the Holy

Spirit who is in you. You have received the Holy Spirit from God. So you do not belong to yourselves, because you were bought by God for a price. So honor God with your bodies" (1 Corinthians 6:19–20).

CHAPTER FOUR

What's the Good Word?

secret

No. 4 – Light verbal candles with words of praise, compassion, and encouragement. Use your words to change lives for the better.

Dr. Paul Faulkner

President, Resources for Living

God says, "A person speaks the things that are in his heart." It is our words that give birth to our identities. Our words don't just represent us; they are us. The words we speak become our hearts and souls . . . our belief systems. It's not surprising that the Bible says so much about our words—they express not just our ideas and thoughts, but who we are. No wonder our words carry such weight and power when we share them with others.

The words of a good person give life,
like a fountain of water.

Proverbs 10:11

The Power of Good in Communication

"**M**ichael, my boy, you might as well forget about being a singer. You'll never be able to sing. You just can't do it."

The little dark-haired Italian boy stared in disbelief at his junior high school music teacher. Not sing? But singing was the only thing he really cared about in life. His dad was a wonderful singer. And he wanted to be a singer too. He had planned to be a great Italian tenor. And his favorite dream was to stand on the hills overlooking Rome, Italy, their family's homeland, and sing "O Sole Mio" with joy and reverence.

Michael ducked his head to hide the tears that leaped into his dark eyes, mumbled something, and walked out of the music room for the last time. The next day he had his class schedule changed to drop music. And he gave up singing forever. The unthinking teacher spoke daunting words that snuffed out the candle of his young dream.

For fifty-three years Michael pursued other things. He built a successful career in international business, becoming a consultant who was highly sought by corporations around the world. He married Betty and cared for his family joyfully and well. And his life was surrounded by friends and associates who loved him. Still, his dream to sing simmered in a recess of his mind, like a slow-cooking soup on a back burner.

On New Year's Eve, 1986, Michael and Betty went to a party at a friend's house. During the course of the evening, Michael met our friend, Charlotte Greeson, a marvelously talented music teacher, vocal coach, and conductor—a warm and sensitive lady.

"I've always wanted to sing," said Michael, "but I can't."

"How do you know you can't?" asked Charlotte.

"Well, I've known it since I was a kid. My junior high music teacher told me so."

"I bet you can sing *now*," said Charlotte smiling confidently. "No boy can sing well when his voice is changing in junior high."

"No, I'm sure I can't. Besides, it's too late—I'm sixty-six years old. But thanks for saying so."

"Michael, in the twenty-five years I've been teaching voice, I've never met anyone of any age that I couldn't teach to sing. I doubt seriously that you're the exception."

The flame of Michael's old dream flickered weakly. "Are you serious?" asked Michael. "Do you really think I could learn to sing at my age?"

"Well, of course you can. You're obviously extremely bright, and besides, I'm a good teacher. Together we'll do well. Anyway, what have you got to lose by trying?"

"When can we start?" asked Michael eagerly.

"Call me Monday," she said, giving him her card, "and we'll set up a lesson schedule."

When Michael came for his first voice lesson the next week, he couldn't even match pitch with the piano. For fifty-three years he had done exactly what his junior high school teacher had told him to do—he'd forgotten about singing. His unused singing voice had to start from scratch, literally.

Before long, though, Michael began to improve. And over the next three years of voice lessons, he showed good ability and amazing determination to sing. He worked hard, and gradually he became an able, if not virtuoso, Italian tenor at age sixty-nine.

On a gentle Texas spring night in 1990, Charlotte was at home watching television with friends. The doorbell rang, and Charlotte went to answer it. Western Union was there to deliver a telegram, which read:

> Charlotte, I just sang "O Sole Mio" from hills above Rome. Stop. My dream has come true. Stop. Thanks for your encouragement. Don't stop. Love, Michael.

The Power of Words

Words matter. What you say impacts others. Michael was the same person inside at age thirteen and age sixty-six. One teacher used *dis*couraging words, the other teacher used *en*couraging words, and they achieved opposite results.

I believe the famous world leader Mohandas Gandhi held the key to the use of good words. The biographer who recorded his life, said this about him: "He often changed human beings by regarding them not as what they were, but as though they were what they wished to be."

Words are life-changing! Words can make or break people. Good words produce good results; bad words produce bad results. Look at what Blaise Pascal, French mathematician, physicist, and philosopher, said: "Cold words freeze people, and hot words scorch them, and bitter words make them bitter, and wrathful words make them wrathful. Kind words also produce their own image on men's souls; and a beautiful image it is. They soothe, and quiet, and comfort the hearer."

Wise King Solomon goes one step farther in describing the power of words: "What you say can mean life or death" (Proverbs 18:21).

People, families, and nations have been built up or destroyed by the words of their leaders. The poisonous words of Germany's Hitler led his people to inflict indescribable evil on other peoples. But the honorable words of Abraham Lincoln led his nation to begin ending human slavery in America.

And who can deny the power of the Word of God that saves us from our sins and leads us into his marvelous grace? His words are true and right and holy. His words guide us into joyful living and away from evil. His Word can translate us from this dark world into heavenly light for all eternity. It is life and hope, if only we accept it. God's Word is truly the ultimate light of the world. As the psalmist said to God in Psalm 119:105: "Your word is like a lamp for my feet and a light for my path."

✧

"Your word is like a lamp for my feet and a light for my path."

✧

Joseph Priestly failed as a preacher and turned to teaching. Once, while on vacation, Joseph happened to meet the esteemed Benjamin Franklin, who was twice his age. Franklin saw great possibilities in Priestly—far more than grade-school teaching, he thought.

"You have just the abilities to write a history of electricity," Franklin told Priestly, "and I will help you start by lending you my books and notes."

Priestly was thrilled and amazed by Franklin's words of encouragement, and he rushed to the task. In a year he had finished the first history of electricity. Then he went on to become a great man of science himself, discovering oxygen and developing the first carbon dioxide fire extinguisher, all thanks to a few words of praise and encouragement from Ben Franklin.

Words . . . simple words . . . had changed his life. Then *his* changed life changed *our* lives. You may never know what your encouraging words result in ultimately. You might change one life or millions of lives with the use of your tongue. So the more often you apply good words to others, the better chance you have of changing the world for good. The more verbal candles you light, the brighter the world will be. Words of hope and cheer can drive away the darkness.

Dr. Scott Stanley, in his twenty-year research at the University of Denver regarding the ingredients necessary to have a successful long-term relationship, has documented the power of words in the marriage relationship. He says, "It takes ten positive comments to make up for just one critical comment. If we can just teach couples to stop tearing each other down with their words when they are in conflict, we've won the battle."

Live Up to It, Or Live It Down

I love the story of the little boy who said to his father, "Let's play darts. I'll throw, and you say, 'Wonderful!' "

All people need encouragement to achieve; they need recognition for their accomplishments. But most people don't make their needs known quite as clearly as this little boy. Instead, they wait patiently, and often in pain, for the rest of us to notice them and offer words of kindness and approval. When they hear the good words they need to hear, life is beautiful, but when they hear hurtful words, life can become ugly. "The right word spoken at the right time is as beautiful as gold apples in a silver bowl" (Proverbs 25:11).

It was 1957. I had just come from a thirteen-year preaching ministry with a large church in Lubbock, Texas, to Los Angeles to serve as president of what was then called George Pepperdine College. It was a stressful time because the college was facing severe financial problems, and I was taking on the biggest challenge of my life.

I was attending my first meeting of college presidents in California—a prestigious group of my peers. The man who introduced me was the influential author of California's higher education plan. In his introduction he said, "We know Dr. Young knows how to build a Sunday school. We don't know if he knows anything about building a college." Those derogatory words stung. I was embarrassed in front of my new peers. The circumstances I faced were discouraging enough without having the added suggestion of the likelihood of failure. And I spent forty years living those words down.

> When destructive words are flung at us, we have a choice: take them to heart, or take them to task.

While it's important for us to offer good words of encouragement and enthusiasm to others, it's equally important that we recognize how others' words affect us and that we respond to those words in constructive ways. When destructive words are flung at us, we have a choice: believe them or ignore them. Live up to them, or live them down. Take them to heart, or take them to task. Just because someone says something to us or about us, that doesn't make it true.

Through the years I have found that most people are too quick to take other people's words to heart without first taking them to task. Here's my personal three-step formula for determining how I will respond to another person's words about me:

1. **Examine its truth.** In all honesty, are the words true?

2. **Live up to it.** If they are true, I will attempt to change my life as needed in accordance with God's Word.

3. **Live it down.** If they are not true, I will move on and try to live so no one else will think of saying them about me in the future.

That third one's the tough one for me. I hate criticism. But in a leadership role, I'm often faced with it. I don't like to think that people can point their fingers at me in derision and be right. I'm always tempted to retaliate and prove them wrong. I want to justify my actions.

I discovered early that defending myself against criticism would cause me to spend all my time in self-justification and little time in constructive work. Then my critics would have something legitimate to criticize about me.

President Abraham Lincoln faced unusually severe criticism much of his life. His advice is still good for us today:

> If I tried to read, much less answer, all the criticism made of me and all the attacks leveled against me, this office would be closed for all other business. I do the best I know how, the very best I can. I mean to keep on doing this, down to the very end. If the end brings me out all wrong, then ten angels swearing I had been right would make no difference. If the end brings me out all right, then what is said against me now will not amount to anything.

Jesus didn't waste his time and energy defending himself against criticism either. He never retaliated by attacking his critics. Rather, he used the occasion to teach and to clarify his mission; then he moved on to minister to those who would listen. He actually taught his followers to "turn the other cheek" to their critics. His great love for lost people and his strong sense of identity in God's purpose could not be shaken by negative words of criticism. He saved his energy to do the good will of his Father.

The three-step formula still works: (1) Look at criticism honestly, (2) change, if necessary, or (3) move on. Don't wallow in the pigpen of self-pity and self-doubt. Don't become incapacitated or inhibited by others' opinions. Be true to yourself and the God who made you. Use his Word as your measuring stick; it's the only one that's completely accurate.

Be Lavish with Praise, Stingy with Criticism

It may be that praise, like gold and diamonds, owes its value to its scarcity, as Samuel Johnson once said, but I prefer to err on the side of giving too much praise, rather than too little.

The wife of an old New Englander named Eb would agree. Old Eb was, like many of his breed, rather stingy with words. He said very little, and then rather grudgingly. One evening he was sitting on the front steps with his wife. The long day's work, the good supper, and the peaceful sights and sounds of dusk must have softened him up. He took his pipe out of his mouth and said, "When I think of what you've meant to me all these years, Judith, sometimes it's almost more than I can stand not to tell you."

✧

"You can't be big and little at the same time. If you're going to be magnanimous, you can't also be stingy."

✧

What about you? Are you lavish or stingy with your praise? When your children come home with a good report card from school, do you take the time to give lavish words of praise and encouragement, or do you just grunt and selfishly go back to your paper? When your husband or wife has achieved some kind of personal goal, like losing five pounds, do you really praise and celebrate that achievement with your mate, or do you just mumble "uh-huh" and keep at your own task?

My father, M. N. Young Sr., used to say to me, "You can't be big and little at the same time. If you're going to be magnanimous, you can't also be stingy." You're either generous with your praise and encouragement, or you're not. You're either openhanded or closefisted, but you can't possibly be both at the same time. If you're magnanimous one moment and stingy the next, you're fickle, and who can depend on a fickle friend? You must choose to be consistently lavish in your honest praise and encouragement. If it's unnatural for you, work at it anyway, because the results will be worth it, both for you and everyone around you.

The Bible teaches in so many places that we are to praise God for his works and his mighty power. We are made in the image of God, and God loves to be praised by us. So, isn't it logical that we, who are created in his image, also need praise from each other? And isn't it logical that we must be the ambassadors of praise from God to other people?

Add Praise to Your Days

Perhaps it's not easy for you to praise others. Maybe you just can't think of things to say or do to encourage people around you. Here are some simple-but-effective suggestions to help add praise to your days. Choose one or more of these to do every day for at least thirty-one days, then you will begin to form the habit of consistent praise.

- Put a note and treat in your mailbox thanking the mail carrier for consistently bringing your mail on time and to the right address.

- Send a congratulatory card to someone who has achieved a personal success, such as losing weight, getting a promotion, or landing a new job.

- Compliment your neighbor for how well he or she manicures the lawn and keeps the neighborhood looking nice.

- Send your child's teacher at school or Sunday school a note and/or small gift saying how much you appreciate the job she's doing with your child's education.

- Call an old friend and say how much you miss being together because of some special trait the friend has (e.g., "I miss your sense of humor").

- Send some flowers to the office staff at your church or your child's school, thanking them for the splendid work they do every day.

- Write a letter to the editor of your local newspaper praising the local police force, the fire department, or the emergency rescue teams.

- Take your child out of school for one day and do something special the child would enjoy just to say how blessed you feel to be his or her parent.

- When you're in public with your spouse, compliment him or her in front of your friends about something important.

- Send some of your child's toys and books that are in good shape to a homeless shelter with a note saying how much you appreciate the work they do.

- Make a construction-paper sign to put up in your child's room that says, "You're the greatest kid in the world!"

- Put a note in your spouse's briefcase that says, "I'm proud of you."

- Tell the people who wash your car how great it looks.

- Call your parents and tell them how fortunate you feel to be their child. Then do the same thing for your grandparents.

- Write a complimentary letter to the supervisor of a clerk or serviceperson who has been particularly helpful to you.

- Order pizza for your office staff as a surprise thank-you for the great work they do.

- Leave an extra-large tip for the serving person who does an outstanding job.

- Tell your loved ones often that they are lovable.

• Say a prayer of praise to God for all the wonderful things he does for you every day: "Thank you, God, for giving me life, health, work to do, and strength to do it."

By the time you do one or more of these every day for a month, you'll begin to think of your own special ways to praise others. And the more you do it, the more you'll enjoy it. Why not start today?

Watch What You Say in Passing

In 1970 Mary graduated from Abilene Christian University and began working on her masters degree in journalism and communication. Her assigned graduate advisor was Dr. Rex Kyker, dean of the graduate school, whom she had never met. On her first and only visit with Dr. Kyker to establish her degree plan, they were discussing whether she should take an extra six-hour graduate course or write a masters thesis to complete her degree.

Dr. Kyker said, "Oh, I definitely think you should do the thesis because you're a writer."

At that point in her life, Mary had never entertained the thought of writing as her career. She'd won a few writing awards in high school and had some articles published in the university newspaper, but that was all. Her undergraduate degree was in business—something practical. Writing was strictly a hobby, nothing more.

After a year in graduate school, Mary landed a job on the personal staff of H. L. Hunt, the oil billionaire, and moved to Dallas. Her job included ghostwriting political comment columns for Mr. Hunt, which were syndicated nationwide under the title *Hunt for Truth*.

Later, Mary took a job in the business world. In her spare time she wrote occasional articles for magazines, had a few poems published, and edited her company newspaper. But writing was still only a hobby. She wouldn't have dreamed of *giving up her day job* to become a full-time freelance writer. And yet, Dr. Kyker's words kept haunting her.

In 1983 Mary began doing freelance work for a Christian publishing company. And when an editorial position became available at the publishing house, she was offered the job. Now, over fifty published books later, Mary's been a full-time freelance writer/editor for almost ten years. As this chapter is being written, two of her books stand at numbers one and three on the bestsellers' list, and her books have sold millions of copies.

Dr. Kyker's words of encouragement, said only in passing, have echoed across millions of lives. Did he do it intentionally? Not really. In fact, years later, when Mary asked him if he remembered what he'd said to her, he didn't. He had simply been doing his job, which included encouraging students to be all they could be.

Rex Kyker went home to God during the writing of this book. At his funeral the family read Mary's tribute to Dr. Kyker from her book *Apple Blossoms*—a gift book for teachers dedicated to Dr. Kyker. His own good words finally came back as good words about himself.

Words said in passing can be powerful . . . life altering . . . life building . . . or life destroying. Be careful what you say in passing! Craft your words to perfectly fill the void in people's lives. Carve them carefully. Mold them. Form them to fit the emotional and spiritual needs of your family and friends. Use your words as pillars upon which people can erect hopes and dreams.

Perhaps you can even learn to toss truthful words of encouragement to people in passing. To the bus driver, say, "You really know how to handle this bus!" To the minister, say, "You touched my life today." To the waitress, say, "I really admire the way you carry all those plates without dropping them." To the checker at the supermarket, say, "You are so courteous to your customers."

It will cost you nothing but a thoughtful moment to help others feel important, appreciated, and admired. Why not be a conduit of praise from God to his world . . . just in passing?

Lead through Encouragement

During the last sixty years of being in a leadership role, I've found four statements that summarize my philosophy of leading people through encouragement. These personal philosophies have worked for me. Perhaps you can adopt them successfully as well.

I LIKE YOU

I don't just *tolerate* you; I *like* you. I've spent enough time and effort to get to know the real you, and I have found something that I sincerely like. Even if I don't necessarily like *everything* about you, I can find *something* about you to like.

I like you. I like your smile, your honesty, or your determination. I like your joy, your compassion, or your gentleness. I like your singing, your free spirit, or your hair. Somewhere, somehow, I have found something about you that I like. And I'll concentrate on that until I find something else about you I like.

I try to approach every person I meet with the attitude that says, "I'm *confident* that I'm going to like you. And if I don't find something right away that I can like, I'm going to keep trying until I discover that place where you and I are on common ground. I just know I'm going to like you."

I have found that attitude to be disarming, even for the toughest critic. I've made friends with hundreds of taxi drivers, waiters and waitresses, elevator operators, airline attendants, and others all over the world by engaging them in friendly conversation to convey that simple, but powerful, message, "I like you."

I ADMIRE YOU

For one reason or another, I admire something about you. Maybe you can build something beautiful with your hands; I admire someone who can do that. I admire your work ethic, your personal discipline, or your ability to handle money well. I admire your talent at arranging flowers, your sincere interest in homeless people, or your patience with your critics.

I have yet to meet a person in whom I cannot find *something* to admire. Sometimes I have to work at it, but there's always something.

My wife's grandfather, F. L. Young, always said good things about people. A friend once said to him, "I'll bet you'd even say something good about the devil."

Grandfather said, "Well, he's very industrious; he's always busy."

There's a hunger in every human heart to be respected and admired. So, it's worth your extra effort to look at people until you find something in them that you can admire. Then you can help them feel the love and admiration God holds for every person he created.

I NEED YOU

The Lord wisely gave each of us different talents and gifts. He didn't give any one of us *all* the talents and gifts. So, we need each other. I need you because you're a capable mechanic, and I'm mechanically challenged. I need you because you know how to comfort me when I'm depressed. I need your cheerfulness, your wisdom, or your hope. I need you to need me. I need you to balance my checkbook, write a poem for me, or sing a song at my office party. I need your friendship and love and care. I need your tuxedo for a black-tie wedding. I need you to pray for me.

Do you remember Aesop's fable titled *The Lion and the Mouse?* The mouse accidentally ran across the nose of the sleeping lion. The lion awoke, roared at the mouse, and caught it by the tail. Just before the lion ate the tiny mouse, the mouse begged, "Please let me go, and someday when you're in trouble, I'll return the favor by helping you."

The lion thought it was hilarious that a wimpy little mouse could ever do anything to help him. In fact, he thought it was so funny that he actually let the mouse go.

A few days later some hunters came into the jungle and managed to trap the lion. They tied him up with strong ropes and secured the ropes to the stakes in the ground to restrain the lion. The lion began to roar loudly over and over. He could not get loose, no matter what he tried. The little mouse heard the lion, recognized his roar, and went to investigate. He found the lion helplessly tied to the stakes in the ground.

Remembering his promise to the lion, the mouse began chewing away at the ropes holding the lion down. Soon he freed the lion. Then he said, "Perhaps now you can see that even a little mouse like me can sometimes help a lion in trouble."

No matter who it is, no matter what their educational or financial level, no matter what kind of clothes they wear, no matter what their nationality or political persuasions, no matter who their parents were or what age they are, you need them. As the old man said to his grandson, "If nothing else, son, you need him as a bad example."

Look for a reason to need people, and they will need you in return.

I WANT TO HELP YOU

The greatest people who have ever lived are helpers. Think about Jesus Christ, whose life was characterized by helping others. Think about Florence Nightingale, the dedicated nurse of the Crimean War. Think about any real hero, and you'll find yourself thinking of someone who worked for the betterment of others.

Several years ago a farmer from southern Illinois, dressed in his overalls, arrived at the Moody Bible Institute and asked if he could look around. Instead of making him wander around on his own, a student was assigned to escort him on an extended tour of the buildings.

The student and everyone else was especially kind to him, although he was a complete stranger. A few days later the institute received a letter expressing thanks for the help and courtesy shown him and commending them for the Christian spirit he had seen in students and faculty. He enclosed a large donation.

Find the best way to help others reach their personal goals, and you'll not only help them, you'll help yourself as well. Any time you lift someone else up, you raise yourself a notch too. As often as you can, say to another person, "I want to help you," or "What can I do to help you?" And then do it! You'll never be sorry.

Cyberspace Compassion?

According to the *Wall Street Journal,* even the funeral industry is going on-line. Cellular phones, video cameras, and computers are now being used to take funeral services to the mourners. Funeral homes routinely videotape services for friends and relatives unable to attend. And one New York funeral home plans to roll out an on-line funeral hookup, so cybermourners can sign on to participate in services and express their condolences on a "chat line." Somehow, it just doesn't seem the same, does it?

On the one hand, it seems almost irreverent to send electronic sympathies, doesn't it? You can't fax a hug. Neither can you hold a friend's hand or wipe away a tear on the Internet. On the other hand, good words of comfort and compassion will likely be welcomed by those in pain, no matter how they arrive. And the Internet is one of the fastest ways to get your compassionate message to a friend or family member, especially if they are far away.

Is this method preferable to a personal touch or a face-to-face conversation? No, but it's certainly better than doing nothing if you are not able to be there in person. After all, is an e-mail condolence so very different from a regular mail condolence, if it comes from the heart? Words of compassion must flow from Christians by whatever means they can devise—cards, letters, phones, faxes, telegrams, and, yes, even e-mail. The computer is only one tool that's available to transmit your message. But it's not the tool that's important, it's the message itself that matters.

Through the years I have made a habit of telephoning the closest family member when I read in the newspaper, or hear otherwise, of the death of a friend. I find a call is a very effective means of expressing sympathy.

By whatever effective means we can find, we must reflect God's words of comfort to others, for he is the God of all comfort. "He comforts us every time we have trouble, so when others have trouble, we can comfort them with the same comfort God gives us" (2 Corinthians 1:4).

Final Words

Gracious words, loving words, kind words, good words—these are the lights that shine into dark places. The word *encourage* simply means to "put courage in" someone else. When we encourage others with good words, we infuse them with the courage to go on. We put in them the nerve to face the darkness without fear. We add backbone and strength to their lives.

Sometimes we encourage others with written words, such as greeting cards, a gift book, or a handwritten note. Sometimes we encourage others with carefully planned speeches, like sermons, motivational talks, or Sunday school lessons. Sometimes we toss courage to others with kind words we speak in passing. Or, perhaps, we even give them a jolt of cybercourage. However we deliver good words of encouragement and cheer to others is right. Whatever verbal candles we light in another's darkness are good.

CHAPTER FIVE

Making Good Grades

secret

No. 5 – Become personally involved in helping, not criticizing, our schools. Encourage literacy and excellence in education—educate for eternity.

Dr. R. Gerald Turner

President,
Southern Methodist University

When it comes to lighting candles in the education arena, one strong administrator, one charismatic teacher, one dedicated parent, or one small group of committed students can take a school mired in despair and transform it into a force for hope and good in the lives of hundreds of people living in desperate conditions.

The mind of a person with understanding gets knowledge;
the wise person listens to learn more.

Proverbs 18:15

The Power of Good in Education

S amuel Taylor Coleridge was once talking with a man who had come to visit him at his home. During their conversation, the man told Coleridge that he didn't believe in giving little children any moral or religious education whatsoever. His theory was that children's minds should not be swayed in any certain direction. He thought children should be allowed to wander mentally free, and when they are old enough, they should then choose their moral and religious opinions for themselves.

Coleridge didn't respond, but after a while he asked the man if he would like to see his garden. The man said he would, and Coleridge took him out into the garden, where weeds of all kinds were on the rampage. The man looked at Coleridge in surprise.

He said, "Why, this is not a garden! There's nothing here but weeds!"

"Well, you see," said Coleridge, "I didn't wish to infringe upon the liberty of the garden in any way. I was just giving the garden a chance to express itself and then choose its own production."

Unfortunately, in America we have neglected the garden of education, especially spiritual education, and weeds of all kinds have grown up—weeds of illiteracy, immorality, crime, and misplaced values. Still, there is hope, if we approach education with aggressive good.

Our Moral Picture

In 1963 prayer was taken out of the public schools, and religious principles were separated from education. According to research from Wallbuilders, the resulting trends that developed in the twenty years immediately following that change in American education are staggering. We know that statistics do not always give the entire picture and that education certainly cannot be blamed for all the deterioration in our society, but these trends are shocking.

- In 1962, the average SAT score was around 985; by 1994 scores had fallen to around 900.

- Sexually transmitted diseases in children ages 10-14 have risen from 14 per 100,000 in 1963 to as high as 66 per 100,000 in 1989.

- Around 240,000 violent crimes were committed in 1961-1962. By 1993, that number had risen to 1.9 million.

- In 1960, only 6 percent of births were to unmarried women. By 1990, the number had risen to 28 percent.

President Theodore Roosevelt summed up what has happened in our country well: "When you educate a man in mind and not in morals, you educate a menace to society."

Dr. Robert Coats, a graduate of Harvard University, who appeared on *Good Morning, America* on January 27, 1997, has done extensive research in what he calls the *moral intelligence* of children.

Dr. Coats explained that children's moral *intelligence* is simply their moral *behavior*. It's not something that can be quantified or tested, but it's a characteristic that is highly developed at a very early age.

Dr. Coats' research found evidence that babies may, in fact, learn some behaviors in the womb, based on the mother's positive or negative behavior patterns during pregnancy. Of great importance is his statement that children look to adult behavior as their model for morality. They do what they see done. And he went on to emphasize that parents, caregivers, and schoolteachers have the most powerful influence for good or evil with children.

✦

"When you educate a man in mind and not in morals, you educate a menace to society."

✦

Read It or Weep

According to government statistics, over ninety million Americans cannot read. That's about 42 percent of the U.S. adult population! Many people can't read medicine labels, street signs, restaurant menus, or even rest room signs. They can't manage a checking account, fill out a job application, or read a picture book to their children. Many people can't read even the most basic, important notices for their lives. That also means that millions of American adults, much less their children, cannot read the Bible—God's Word for lighting our way. Many of them are fumbling around in the darkest kind of darkness—spiritual darkness. They are lost and can't read the signs that point them to the place of safety. Evil is winning these people over one at a time by default.

Millions of adults are *functionally illiterate.* In other words, they don't read well enough to function properly in our society. They have to get help from family members or friends with everyday papers and magazines, documents, and simple reading tasks. The *average* American adult reads on a fourth-grade level or below.

The National Institute for Literacy reports that every year one million students drop out of school, lacking reading, writing, and fundamental job skills. Couple that with information from the U.S. Department of Education that says "under education is the biggest predictor of illiteracy" and that "70 percent of native English-speaking illiterates did not finish high school," and you can see what a serious problem we face.

It's not a crime to be illiterate. But it's estimated that 85 percent of the juveniles who appear in court *are* illiterate, 75 percent of the unemployed are illiterate, and 60 percent of prison inmates are illiterate. It's not a crime to be illiterate, but those who are illiterate may turn to crime. The two seem to be related. I am reminded of Victor Hugo's quote, "He who opens a school, closes a prison."

The United States ranks twentieth among the twenty-two industrialized nations in literacy. Look at these staggering statistics:

- Some 44 percent of American adults never read a book, including the Bible, in the course of a year.

- Upon high school graduation, the average student has watched fifteen thousand hours of television, compared with twelve thousand hours spent in all school classes.

- Average middle-school-age children read books for pleasure for no more than five *minutes* a day. But 27 percent of all nine-year-olds watch more than six *hours* of television a day.

- Over 80 percent of U.S. colleges and universities have to provide remedial courses for freshmen because high schools are often issuing graduation certificates to seniors who can't actually read or write well.

- Ten percent of Americans read 80 percent of the available books.

- Only one out of ten Christians ever visits a Christian bookstore.

Literacy—A Spiritual Issue

I am convinced that illiteracy is far more than an educational problem; it's a spiritual problem, and one that we as Christians have, for the most part, ignored or overlooked. Like the Dark Ages of history, what we need is an age of enlightenment. We need good education to light the way again. We need more than an educational system that teaches reading and writing; we need it to teach morals and values as well. Plenty of intellectually astute people are moral degenerates and valueless citizens. The putrid pile of pornography that litters our country proves that authors with honed writing skills can be spiritually corrupt, spewing out rancid reading material to society. And now, by computer and telephone, pornography is multiplying its impact.

We need to teach goodness and righteousness and morality. We need to be attacking the darkness with the light.

But where can we begin to turn the tide of illiteracy? We should encourage organizations like Project Literacy and applaud Oprah Winfrey's television emphasis on reading. And each of us can do our part as well. As Barbara Bush did with her children and grandchildren, we need to start at home building a love of learning. There is no greater way than to read to children from their infancy and, later, listen to them read. A father who reads Bible stories and other stories at bedtime gives his children a priceless legacy.

I have heard my wife, Helen, say that she remembers her father reading to her and helping her memorize Scripture before she was six years old. It's a great lifetime inheritance.

Literacy and the Bible

Let's take a look at the Bible, for instance. While many Christians cling to the translations we grew up reading, we must be realistic about the spread of God's Word. If people can't read and understand the Word for themselves, Satan wins. God told us to *study* his Word

93

in order to be approved by him. How can people study who cannot read?

I mentioned that the average American adult reads on a fourth-grade level. Compare their reading *ability* with the reading *levels* of the Bible versions we have traditionally used:

- King James Version - 12th-grade level
- New American Standard Bible - 11th-grade level
- The Amplified Bible - 11th-grade level
- Revised Standard Version - 11th-grade level
- New International Version - 7.8-grade level
- Today's English Version - 7.3-grade level

Average American adults *cannot* read and understand these versions for themselves. It's not that they don't *want* to, they simply are incapable of it, just as an average fourth-grade pupil is unable to understand a twelfth-grade calculus book. We buy our young children picture books that are appropriate for young children. Each page has only a few simple words on it, because we know that's all the child can grasp. And yet, when it comes time to buy those same young children Bibles, we give them the King James Version in a sweet pink or blue cover, even though they can't possibly read or understand it. All they can do is carry it around.

At every age level in children's lives, if they are educated properly, they are capable of learning more and at higher reading levels. It's imperative that we provide God's Word accurately for them at *every* level. We need to come to grips with the needs of the people, just as the scholars did in King James' day. They wanted the average people on the sixteenth-century streets to be able to read the Word and understand it for themselves. The King James Version was the answer in that day and age. It was written in sixteenth-century English—the language of the people on the street.

Today we need Bible translations that are carefully and accurately translated into the language of twenty-first century people. One advertisement that depicts this well shows King James in his royal robes and crown with this quote: "If King James were alive today, he would read the NIV." It's marvelous that we have the availability of many new biblical manuscripts, which give our scholars today the ability to translate the Scriptures more accurately than ever before. And I'm pleased that Christian publishers are addressing this spiritual need for greater understanding. I applaud the easy-to-read Bible translations and Bible study tools. Compare, for instance, the ability of fourth-grade readers—both children and adults—to the reading levels of these newer contemporary-English translations:

- International Children's Bible - 3.8-grade level
- The New Century Version - 4.7-grade level
- Contemporary English Version - 5.4-grade level
- New American Bible - 6.6-grade level

I celebrate these educational and spiritual breakthroughs. The light will shine brightly because of greater spiritual comprehension.

For the Love of Reading

Since reading is the basis of many other kinds of learning, I'd like to suggest some ways to help you stimulate a love of reading, and thus learning, in the people around you, both children and adults.

- Read the Bible regularly. Let others see you reading it. Read it aloud so they can hear you reading it. Let them read it aloud, too, if they can.

- Take time to read to children (and adults) regularly. *Make* time!

- Encourage people to talk about what they're learning and reading. Have open discussions about new topics of learning.

- Have plenty of *good* reading materials around the house or office so they're handy for spare moments.

- Create places where it's easy for people to read: comfortable chairs, good lighting, privacy, good books or magazines to choose from.

- Take regular family trips to your local Christian bookstore to find good reading materials for each person on his or her own reading level.

- Go as a family to the public library and the church library. Help each person secure a library card to use often.

- Lead your family in building up the church library by donating Christian books in good condition.

- Carry a book with you in the car, in your purse or pocket, to read during waiting times (at the doctor's office, in line at the store, in traffic jams, waiting for your food in a restaurant, on airplanes, trains, or buses).

- Give good books, books on tape, and magazine subscriptions as gifts for birthdays, Christmas, and other times.

- Reread a good book you loved as a child, then share it with your own children, grandchildren, nieces, nephews, or neighbors.

- Sponsor "Story Time" for the children around you. Announce that "Story Time" will be held at a certain time each week. Serve a healthy snack for the children to enjoy while you read.

- Take your family to a book signing by a local or well-known author. Try to talk to the author about the book.

- Instead of buying flowers to honor special people, consider buying good books and donating them to your church or public library in their honor.

- Write positive reviews of good Christian books for your church bulletin to help encourage others to read them.

- Have a regular family reading time. Take turns choosing what book is to be read next. You might combine the reading time with family devotional time at breakfast or before bedtime.

- Help sponsor an annual book fair at your church so that parents, teachers, and children can see what Christian books are available.

- Use a daily family devotional, such as *Power for Today*, and let your children take turns reading the devotionals.

Get involved! Be a library-card-carrying, bookmark-waving reader. And encourage others around you to be readers and learners too. As Daniel Webster said, "If we work upon marble, it will perish; if on brass, time will efface it; if we rear temples, they will crumble into dust; but if we work upon immortal minds, and imbue them with principles, with the just fear of God and love of our fellow men, we engrave on those tablets something that will brighten to all eternity."

The home-schooling movement has over 1.2 million school-age children being trained by their parents. They score significantly higher on standardized achievement tests than do their public school counterparts. In all education, hard work and parental involvement lead to superior results.

University-Level Education

I have spent most of my active career in Christian education and most of that at Pepperdine University. I've seen it transformed from a small, struggling college in the Watts area of downtown Los Angeles to a multicampus university with its undergraduate Seaver College and School of Law gracing the hills overlooking the Malibu coastline.

When Ronald Reagan was governor of California in the 1970s, he appointed me to the Coordinating Council on Higher Education of California, which coordinated the educational programs for all the private and public colleges and universities of the State. Ronald Reagan believed in the value of good education, and he was willing to give his valuable time and energy to support it, both publicly and privately. He shared the dream of Pepperdine's founder that good education must include values.

Governor Reagan visited Pepperdine and spoke to our students, faculty, and alumni a number of times. On February 9, 1970, he spoke at our "Birth of a College Dinner" to launch the building of the Malibu campus. We rented the huge ballroom of the Century Plaza Hotel in Los Angeles, even though most people thought it was far too large for a dinner for such a small school. But God blessed us with a sellout crowd. In fact, when we knew it would be an overflow crowd, we also rented the ballroom at the Beverly Wilshire Hotel down the street. Governor Reagan spoke twice—before dinner at the Century Plaza and then after dinner at the Beverly Wilshire. We will always be grateful for his generous support and the grand way he christened Pepperdine's Malibu campus.

The Dream

Pepperdine grew out of the vision of a man born in a one-room home in the rich farmlands of Kansas in 1886. His youth was influenced by the deep religious commitment of his parents, who were members of a frontier religious movement designed to restore Christianity as it was in the first century. Young George Pepperdine, after gaining a business-college education, was first employed with a local gas company at a salary of six dollars a week.

George was a thoughtful and visionary young man. He had observed with curiosity that automobiles in 1906 were sold in stripped condition; few came equipped with tops, windshields, or bumpers. If the owners were to have headlights, they had to purchase oil-burning lamps and hang them on the fronts of the cars. George pondered the possibility of establishing an auto-parts business to fill an obvious need of the consumer. But newly married, he was faced with domestic obligations too. His job as a bookkeeper at a Kansas City garage paid him a relatively comfortable fifteen dollars a week. That was security, but George Pepperdine was a risk-taker. He had five dollars and a good idea. The idea was that the horseless carriage needed additional parts.

His initial five-dollar investment was used to buy five hundred penny postcards to advertise his new mail-order auto parts business to American automobile owners. George sent these cards, which listed his retail prices, to all car owners in the Kansas City area. When the cash orders came in, he purchased the items from a wholesaler, packaged them at home with his wife Lena's help, and mailed them to the buyers. Thus, the huge Western Auto Supply chain was born.

Years later, George Pepperdine moved to California and started a chain of stores here. He successfully weathered the depression and finally sold his business in 1939. By that time he had established 170 stores in eleven western states with numerous associate stores selling Western Auto products.

When he realized he was a multimillionaire at age fifty, George Pepperdine felt a great sense of responsibility to God, to his country, and to the society that had supported him. He had a generous heart and had already established a nonprofit eleemosynary foundation in 1931 to provide gifts to religious, charitable, and educational organizations. He had given generously to churches, the YMCA, the Boy Scouts, and he had established a girls' home. But he longed to do something even more significant.

He considered the possibility of establishing a college. And after careful investigation, he decided to proceed. George said this about his new venture: "I have in mind a privately endowed, four-year liberal arts college, an institution of higher learning where any worthy young person, regardless of his religion or financial standing, can get an education. And I want it to be a college that is academically sound, based on Christian faith. Is that too much to ask?"

It was *not* too much to ask, and in the fall of 1937, *Time* magazine made this announcement: "Last week George Pepperdine was bubbling with plans for a new enterprise to be called George Pepperdine

College. He has thirty-four acres of land on Los Angeles' flat south side, and plans for ten buildings, of which four, low and glass-sided, will be ready for use this autumn."

Pepperdine College, whose acreage at 79th Street and Vermont Avenue was purchased for $150,000, was a brave new experiment launched in the midst of the depression by one man. It was located in a bright, new, middle-class suburb, quite a distance by streetcar from downtown Los Angeles. There were no freeways. And the war clouds in Europe were threatening.

Still, there was a spirit of unbounded optimism among faculty, administrators, and students. There were 167 eager students from many states. Department chairmen were paid an enviable $3,000 per year. And there was a million-dollar endowment. George Pepperdine College gained *full* accreditation just seven months after its founding.

Through the years, Pepperdine had its ups and downs. We survived the wars. We survived being in the center of the Watts riots. We survived major financial stresses. We survived because, through it all, we honored George's dream of having a Christian environment where students from all backgrounds could learn at the highest academic and moral levels. We could never have survived without that dream.

The school grew rapidly. We added the Graduate School of Education and Psychology; then we added the Graduate School of Business. After that we acquired the School of Law. In 1971, Pepperdine College became Pepperdine University and moved its undergraduate Seaver College to the Malibu campus. It was an exciting time.

I have often said that happiness is being proud of your successors. Today at Pepperdine our seven thousand students benefit from a long history of dedication to educating people who realize that education calls for a life of service. Thanks to the example and leadership of such great administrators as Bill Banowsky, Howard Whiton, Charles Runnels, David Davenport, as well as talented and dedicated deans and faculty, our graduates go out year after year to shine like stars in the darkness of our world. And we at Pepperdine strive to educate their successors because there will always be darkness that needs light.

Right and Rights

The forces of ignorance and evil have attacked our educational system, it's true. But lighting candles of goodness is still the key to overcoming this evil. In truth, if we are uneducated people, we can make little impact on the world. Either we are leaders, or we are led. Either we are winners, or we are won. Either we overcome evil, or evil overcomes us. There is no in-between.

In the game of tennis, there's an area on the court referred to by players as no-man's land. In other words, no man should be caught there because he simply can't defend himself or be aggressive from that place on the court. It's a loser's position. The opponent's returns can easily sail past no-man's land, and a player cannot hit the ball effectively from that area.

For two decades now, education and educators have been caught in no-man's land. We can't seem to go forward, and we surely don't want to go backward. Politicians and parents are screaming for higher standards of education because we're running behind other industrialized nations. Administrators, teachers, and boards of education are under pressure to produce higher SAT and ACT scores. Universities are bemoaning the poor academics of the students who come to them as freshmen. And industry complains that people entering the work force lack basic technical skills, basic honesty, and a basic work ethic.

> ✧
>
> Either we overcome evil, or evil overcomes us. There is no in-between.
>
> ✧

At the same time, educators have been told that they can't discipline, can't teach morals and values, can't mention the Bible or religion, have to pass students even when they're not making the grade, and certainly can't pray. Some have been convinced that they're the victims and the students are the victors. They're plagued with lawsuits, parental vehemence, student disrespect, threats from advocacy groups, lack of administrative support, and insufficient budgets. They're made to believe that they basically have no rights as educators. Many work longer hours for less pay than other professionally trained workers in America. They feel at the mercy of the system.

In reality, many of the threats and innuendoes teachers hear are based on legal myths and false information. And guess who promotes false information and legal myths? Our old enemy—the devil himself—the one who wants teachers to feel powerless, threatened, and victimized.

In truth, the courts and legal system of the United States have been a great friend to educators and education. The Supreme Court, especially, has traditionally and consistently upheld the rights and privileges of educators, in spite of what we have falsely been led to believe. We are often *kept in the dark* by the press about rulings that support and uphold goodness and right, but when evil scores some small victory, the media often plays it to the hilt.

Fortunately, through the efforts of such organizations as the Rutherford Institute, the truth is finding its way back into public and legal view. Founded in 1982 by John W. Whitehead, author and attorney, the Rutherford Institute is a nonprofit, international civil liberties legal and educational organization that defends religious persons whose constitutional rights have been violated. These services are provided free of charge. The institute also educates religious persons on exercising their religious rights in their cultures.

The Rutherford Roots

"Will you help me?"

The schoolteacher's question struck a resonant chord deep inside attorney John Whitehead. The young lawyer had moved to Los Angeles a few months earlier in search of spiritual answers at a seminary. The teacher who asked the question had been reprimanded by public school officials for telling her students why she wore a cross necklace. Now she was asking John for something more than he had bargained for.

John helped the young Los Angeles schoolteacher by persuading her principal to respect her constitutional rights. But John would hear that same simple question thousands of times in the years ahead. His determination to help spiritual people led to the founding of the Rutherford Institute.

John spent months researching and writing about the common misconceptions concerning the relationship between church and state. He developed firsthand experience about how distorted legal views were hurting many religious people. He described it this way:

> To my astonishment, I found that many religious people are afraid to live by their beliefs in public for fear of discrimination. Some of their concerns may have been due to the fact that religious people had mostly withdrawn from society and were not participating in their culture. But some of this fear was due to discrimination, which actively seeks to bar religious people and their ideas from full participation in public life.
>
> As I looked into these matters, I discovered, in story after story, that a whole generation of religious people was being systematically disenfranchised from their rights in a free nation. I also realized that most of the people who needed legal help could not afford to pay legal fees. They were suffering a loss of their freedom because they couldn't afford to stand up for what they believed in a court of law. Something had to be done.

In the beginning, one man answered a need by putting his faith into action for the good of education. Today, John Whitehead and the Rutherford Institute are joined by hundreds of attorneys who are ready to pay the price of living out their faith. Whitehead has established a network of state, regional, and international affiliates to defend constitutional freedoms of Christians, such as teachers, around the world. In 1996 alone they handled over nine thousand requests for legal information and assistance.

Reclaiming Lost Ground

Contrary to public opinion and information, Christians still *have* the right and *are* right to be Christians in the public schools or anywhere else in this country. In fact, there is nothing education needs more desperately than Christian educators working in the public sector. We are not prohibited from being who we are, even though the word on the street says differently.

This persecution of Christian educators is only one of the many forms of persecution Christians face today in America. This is the front line of battle. This is day-to-day, face-to-face combat with the enemy. We just haven't called it that; rather, we've simply sat back and accepted whatever persecution Satan and his forces wanted to hand out to us.

✧

"Protection of the rights of the oppressed demands an aggressive and activist philosophy."

✧

A popular myth invoked by Christians and non-Christians alike to justify their refusal to stand against immoral state acts has been the assertion that Christ and the apostles were pacifists. Not true! Jesus was not silent against injustice. He felt free to criticize Jewish civil leaders (John 8:18–23), and he called the Roman-appointed Herod Antipas a "fox" (Luke 13:32). Jesus whipped the moneychangers and chased them out of the temple (John 2:12–17). And Christ is ultimately portrayed in the book of Revelation as exercising righteous vengeance on the secular state. Jesus was no coward! He opposed evil in all situations.

It's time for us, as Christians, to get back on the attack. We have to reclaim the ground we've lost in the battle for morality and goodness in our schools. We have to go back on the offensive, for the sake of the kids, for the sake of our families, for the sake of our country . . . for the sake of our souls. As John Whitehead points out, "Protection of the rights of the oppressed (including Christian educators) demands an aggressive and activist philosophy."

I so strongly believe in this principle that I helped begin the Christian Higher Education Foundation, which is comprised of retired presidents and chancellors of Christian universities and colleges to promote Christian higher education. Our goals include helping churches become responsible for seeing that every high school graduate who wants to go to college can go. We also provide fund-raising seminars to help Christian schools provide scholarships for students who need them. It's our hope that we can lead an aggressive charge in the battle for good education.

Our Report Card

If report cards were issued to nations, I'd be afraid to take ours home to Daddy right now. The truth is, we've flunked Education 101 in America. And yet, I say anything that can go wrong can go right again. We can pump goodness back into education. We can *make the grade* as a nation—if we begin righting the wrongs, fixing what's broken, and doing what's doable to put education back on its pedestal.

Some education "experts" say we should throw out the entire system and completely start over. I take issue with that concept, because the educational system didn't get broken all at one time. It didn't fall from its pedestal like an expensive vase and shatter into a million pieces. Rather, it has gradually eroded over the years and, in my opinion, it can be rebuilt gradually. But we have to start rebuilding. We can't just sit with folded hands waiting for other people to take the lead. We have to do the good that *we* can do. We have to go on the offensive and light candles of good in the darkness.

Jesus was often called the Master Teacher. He spent his entire ministry educating others. He wanted his followers to learn and not be ignorant of God's will for them. He believed in educating his disciples about goodness and right living. He eventually died so that goodness would be victorious over evil eternally. He lit the candle of good education. Now, it's up to us to keep it burning.

CHAPTER SIX

Good Morning, Darling

secret

No. 6 – Christian faith is the strongest foundation for the home; and love, loyalty, and commitment are the building blocks.

Dr. H. Norman Wright

Marriage and Family Counselor,
Author

It's time to look at our families to see what's right with them, rather than what's wrong; to discover what's working and going well, rather than what isn't; to identify the potential of each person, praise God for it, and encourage its development to the fullest. As Norvel suggests, let's become believers of what can be in our families rather than becoming stuck in the past.

Wicked people die and they are no more,
but a good person's family continues.

Proverbs 12:7

The Power of Good in Your Family

Michael Kit Demcheshen, a Ukrainian boy of fourteen, lived in Suhodol, Poland, when World War II broke out. He was one of six children in a family living in a small, out-of-the-way village. While his family was poor, they had great love for each other and were very close. They worked together, played together, and stayed together.

In July 1942, Michael was suddenly abducted from his home by the German Civil Authority and put on a private farm in Austria to work. He remained there in servitude until the war was over in May 1945. Then he spent two years in various displaced-persons camps in Austria, mostly working for English military motorpools.

Michael had no contact with his family after their letters stopped coming in 1944. He tried to contact them, but without success. He concluded that they had most likely been lost during the war.

So, in 1947, through the International Refugee Organization, he applied for immigration to Venezuela, South America. He was taken to Germany where he spent six weeks waiting for a boat to Venezuela.

Alone at age nineteen, Michael spent two years in Caracas working to survive in a foreign country where the language and customs were strange to him. It was in Caracas that he met Ledford and Mildred Hubbard, an American couple temporarily living in Venezuela. He became like a son to the Hubbards, and they were like parents to him. So, the Hubbards decided to help Michael. When they returned to the United States, they made arrangements for Michael to come and stay with them.

On November 16, 1949, at age twenty-one, Michael came to the United States on a student visa and began attending college. Four years later, on June 20, 1953, he married Violet Baxter. In March 1954 Michael was granted permanent residence in America. And on September 8, 1955, Michael Demcheshen became a United States citizen.

Michael and Violet worked and raised their happy family through the years. Eventually they retired in Okmulgee, Oklahoma, where they are still living.

In the early fall of 1996, a young Ukrainian girl came to the States as an exchange student to go to college. She was living with a family in Wellston, Oklahoma, who knew Michael and Violet. Michael and the girl talked about the Ukraine, and Michael told her his life story.

The girl's father is a professional musician in the Ukraine and travels to towns and villages entertaining the people. Michael asked her, the next time she wrote to her father, to ask him to see if any people named Demcheshen still lived in Suhodol the next time he was there. And he gave her the names of his parents and brothers and sisters.

In October 1996 a letter came from the girl's father. He had found all of Michael's family alive and well in the city of Lviv, about thirty-six kilometers from Suhodol. Michael's younger sister still lives in the old family house. Although Michael's parents are deceased, he has discovered his five original siblings, and three more he had never known because they were born after he was taken away. He has also found dozens of nieces and nephews he has never met. In all, there are about eighty Demcheshens in Suhodol and Lviv!

On November 4, 1996, after fifty-four years of believing his entire family was dead and they believing that *he* was dead, Michael talked to one of his nephews—a doctor in Lviv. Although he struggled with the little-used language of his youth, the telephone reunion was sweet indeed. A few days later he talked to his sister (the doctor's mother). At long last, Michael has his family back.

Michael and Violet traveled to the Ukraine in April 1997 to be reunited with his long-lost family. And what a reunion it was! Every photograph from the trip shows hugging, smiling people.

Home. Family. Nothing is more powerful than the magnetic pull of home and family. It's no mistake that "God gives the lonely a home" (Psalm 68:6). He knew that we would need the love and support of other people—people who share in our birth, our growing up, our maturing, our aging, and our death, people who are bone of our bone and flesh of our flesh, people who are related to us in spirit and heart, people who will love and care for us, no matter what happens. These very special people are called *family.*

> ✧
>
> "God gives the lonely a home."
>
> ✧

Since World War II, the sweet words *home* and *family* have taken an incredible beating in our country. Campaigns for individual freedom and autonomy have brought family alienation. Lax premarital behavior, soaring divorce rates, families in conflict and crisis, demands for alternate lifestyles, lack of spiritual leadership, the changing workplace, and other elements have threatened the very structure of family life and, thus, America itself. The darkness has crept closer and closer to the very heart of our lives and nation.

And yet, I can now see the light dawning. Goodness is once again on the rise in families and homes, like the sun rising in the early morn of a new day. All through the years there have been families who have lit candles of loyalty and sacrifice to preserve and solidify the family. There have also been churches upholding God's Word on the sanctity and permanence of marriage, as well as the responsibilities, mutual love, and devotion of parents and children. But the darkness has been very invasive, and many of our individual candles need to be relighted.

Great organizations like Focus on the Family, Family Restoration Network, Promise Keepers, Faith in Families, Adopt-a-Family, and others are reigniting the flames of hope for parents and children everywhere. God in his heaven must be pleased to see many of his people awakening to the desperate condition of families, both inside and outside the church, and taking initiative in giving their children moral and spiritual guidance.

Family Reunions

A few years ago, Helen and I hosted a family reunion of the descendants of the pioneer Texas preacher, Fountain Livingston Young, and his wife, Mattie Higgins Young—Helen's maternal grandparents. (Yes, *her* ancestors were named Young too.)

Over fifty family members came from across the nation. They came from North Carolina to Oregon to attend the two-day celebration. Included were four of the surviving five Young children, all in their not-so-young eighties and nineties. Helen's grandparents actually had thirteen children, all of whom lived to be at least fifty years old. Helen and Dr. F. W. Mattox, founding president of Lubbock Christian University, are two of the seven children of Irene Young Mattox, the eldest of the thirteen.

The reunion was a tremendous experience, filled with speeches of tribute, reminiscences of childhood joys and sorrows, struggles and triumphs. There were humorous anecdotes of the past and hopes and dreams for the future of the clan. And thanksgiving to God for his grace and strength was woven through it all. Memories were shared of stern discipline, a strong work ethic, and the tender love of their parents for God and each other. They spoke of the desire to excel. Their parents gave them a burning ambition to learn, which drove them, with little or no money, to work their way to advanced degrees at Harvard, the University of Chicago, the University of Texas, and other places. The younger children were then helped through college by the older ones.

They read letters from their mother, Mattie, and played tapes from Irene, which made us all cry. The four original Youngs sat as a panel to answer questions from the younger generation. With openness they spoke of conflict, disappointment, and deprivations, but also of fun and the deeper joys of faith. What a privilege to share memories, to implant traditions, to inspire duty, self-esteem, and love. It was wonderful!

In my opinion, what we need all across America is a giant family reunion. We need families to be reunited in love, in spirituality, in hope, and in joy. We need to be reunited in determination to rebuild our families in the image of the inseparable bond of Christ and the Godhead. Since families today are not held together by coercion from without, we must develop a powerful cohesion that glues us together from within, so no force can pull us apart.

> ✧
>
> We must develop a powerful cohesion that glues us together from within, so no force can pull us apart.
>
> ✧

Spiritual Superglue

What is the missing ingredient in families today? Where did we get off track? How did the darkness gain such a hold on our family lives?

The missing ingredient in most broken and damaged families is the spiritual one, in which the commitment of two people in Christ forms the foundation and bond for a stable and successful home. Christ is the superglue that sticks families together for life. Without him, there is little chance of lasting cohesion.

A friend of mine says it reminds her of the first guitar she ever owned when she was a junior in high school. She bought it with six books of S&H Green Stamps, which took her more than two years to save. When it finally arrived in a cardboard box, she had to assemble it herself. She was so proud of that inexpensive Kay guitar, and she did eventually learn to play it, even though the strings were so high off the fingerboard that her fingers bled from trying to hold them down. She persisted until she could play well enough to accompany herself singing.

The following summer she took the guitar with her to camp, where she spent ten weeks as a Christian counselor. The first time it rained, her guitar came all to pieces. When the glue got a little damp, it just wouldn't hold the guitar together anymore. And she ended up with a pile of wood, strings, and tuning pegs that would no longer make music.

Doesn't that sound like many families today? They use the wrong kind of glue to hold themselves together. Instead of Christ, they use the glues of materialism or accomplishment or recognition. Then, the first time it rains, they come unglued. And when the music dies, they end up in divorce court.

When that guitar came unglued, though, my friend didn't give up music. She didn't quit playing. She just saved up her money and bought a new guitar of better quality construction. She got one with stronger glue so that she could keep singing, rain or no rain.

And our families today need to do the same thing. When the rains come down, we need to keep singing because the glue of Christ holds us together, no matter what happens. Instead of dashing down to divorce court, we need to apply more glue and stick it out together. As Ivan Stewart, founder and director of the worldwide Campaigns for Christ, says to campaign workers, "God's people and God's weather go together." And we must learn to weather family storms together, the way a family is meant to do.

Stay in the Boat!

Think about Noah and his family. Talk about rain! But they stuck together through the worst kind of weather in a boat full of smelly animals for months. Can you imagine what they must have had to put up with in the ark? But while things might have been bad *inside*, they knew that *outside* the ark was far worse. If they got fed up and decided to leave their family, their only choice was death by drowning.

I'm convinced that things haven't really changed much since the time of Noah. Families are meant to stick together, through thick and thin, through pain and gain, through sunshine and rain. But when the floodwaters are deepest, we need to stay in the boat. When we get so frustrated with each other we're ready to scream, we need to stay in the boat. When we think that the only way to survive is to leave, we need to commit to stay in the boat. All the chemistry between two people, all the compatibility, all the cooperation, all the communication will go down the drain without this commitment.

Noah and his family spent years building their boat. They built it according to God's standards and blueprints. They used the right kind of wood, pegs, and pitch to hold it together. But the fact is, when the flood overwhelmed the entire world, what held their boat together was God himself. Because they had followed his plan and obeyed his commands, *he* held them together when the going got tough. He kept them afloat. He kept them safe and dry. They stayed in the boat . . . together, and finally, God landed them on the mountaintop. Finally, they saw the rainbow. Only then were they able to begin again, create a whole new life, and move on from the heartaches of the past.

✧

When we think that the only way to survive is to leave, we need to stay in the boat.

✧

115

Christ is the spiritual superglue for families today. If we follow his commands and teachings about families, when the floodwaters rise, he will hold us together. He will keep our families afloat. He will keep us safe and dry . . . if we stay in the boat.

A Few Good Men and Women

Noah found favor in the eyes of the Lord because he was a *good* man. In fact, he was the only good man God could find on earth. And because Noah had consistently been a good man, God rescued him and his family from the flood. What the world needs now is more *good* men. That's the cry of Promise Keepers, the dynamic men's movement. Our families will be kept safe from the storms of life, in large part, through our application of goodness to our spouses and children. Good men are the most powerful catalysts for creating good families, just as God appointed them to be. The Yale scholar, William Lyon Phelps, told his students: "The highest happiness on earth is a happy Christian family. Every man who has a happy family is a successful man, even if he has failed in everything else. And every man whose family is a failure is not a successful man, even if he has succeeded in everything else."

✧

If you're not a Christian at home, you are not a Christian.

✧

Good women are essential too. In truth, it's often good women who keep their husbands and children on the right track. Most of the noble characters and fine leaders of history have had good, God-fearing wives and/or mothers.

We are told, for instance, that President George Washington's mother was pious and that writer Sir Walter Scott's mother was a lover of poetry and music. But the mother of Rome's cruel dictator, Nero, was a murderess, and the dissolute Lord Byron's mother was a proud and violent woman.

I urge you to place greater emphasis on your family relationships. Attack your family with goodness. Be good to your spouse, your children, and your parents. We each have only one family by blood, given to us by God. We should cherish and nourish it. It takes effort, initiative, patience, perseverance, forgiveness, and charity. In fact, family is the best of all places to practice the Christian virtues. If you're not a Christian at home, you are not a Christian.

Reach out to your extended family too. Show concern and love to your aunts, uncles, cousins, and in-laws. Take time for family. Make special occasions, such as birthdays and holidays, major events. Keep up with family members. Use the telephone, revive the lost art of letter writing, communicate by e-mail, visit those you can every time you can. Sponsor a family reunion, where the best of your heritage, especially your spiritual heritage, can be passed on from generation to generation.

Kids, Kindness, and Kudos

Pablo Casals, world-renowned cellist, once described the duty of families toward children in this way:

> Each second we live is a new and unique moment of the universe, a moment that will never be again . . . And what do we teach our children? We teach them that two and two make four, and that Paris is the capital of France.
>
> When will we also teach them what they are?
>
> We should say to each of them: Do you know what you are? You are a marvel! You are unique. In all the years that have passed, there has never been another child like you. Your legs, your arms, your clever fingers, the way you move.
>
> You may become a Shakespeare, a Michaelangelo, a Beethoven. You have the capacity for anything. Yes, you are a marvel. And when you grow up, can you then harm another who is, like you, a marvel?

You must work—we all must work—to make the world worthy of its children.

In my long experience with parents and children in the field of education, I see a lot of regret from parents. They regret that they spent so much time working for money and so little time working with their children. They regret that they allowed their children to do just as they pleased, rather than doing what pleased the Lord. They regret that they demanded so little respect from their children, and now their children show them so little respect. They regret that their children are actually following in their footsteps—footsteps of dishonesty, materialism, selfishness, and lack of spirituality. They regret that they have not been the good parents they should have been, and now their children are not the good children they wish they were. They regret that their children are exactly what they, as parents, have helped them to become.

I often hear parents say things like, "If I had it to do over again, I'd do this or that." Sadly, they don't have it to do over again. We only get one shot at being the right kind of parents to our children. But if we do it right, once is enough. Diane Loomans put it this way in her short article titled, "If I Had My Child to Raise Over Again":

> If I had my child to raise all over again,
> I'd fingerpaint more, and point the finger less.
> I'd do less correcting, and more connecting.
> I'd take my eyes off my watch, and watch with my eyes.
> I would care to know less, and know to care more.
> I'd take more hikes and fly more kites.
> I'd stop playing serious, and seriously play.
> I'd run through more fields, and gaze at more stars.
> I'd do more hugging, and less tugging.
> I would be firm less often, and affirm much more.
> I'd build self-esteem first, and the house later.
> I'd teach less about the love of power,
> And more about the power of love.

But you *don't* have your child to raise all over again. A missionary friend of mine in Thailand often says, "You only go around once in life, and this is no dress rehearsal." It's now or never. Do it now, or forget it. We don't get "overs" in family life and child rearing. We have to take the time now, because this time will not come again. Do it right now and celebrate later, or do it wrong now and regret it forever.

The fact is, children need kindness and kudos. They need goals and dreams to chase. They need hugs and smiles and unconditional love. They need to be part of a family circle that cannot be broken, regardless of the blows it suffers.

Lost Childhood

Young children are so busy today learning to defend themselves in karate classes, playing the violin at age four in Suzuki lessons, and improving their preschool computer skills that they literally have no time to play or to learn to share and to care and to serve. We push them to excel in academics and demand that they be number one on the sports field . . . and that's all before they even start to school! By the time they are seven years old, they're already taking pills for stress. They rarely get to experience the carefree days of childhood.

When do your kids or grandkids get to chase butterflies and fireflies? When do they walk along a quiet creek bank and pick up rocks for their collections? When do they have time to climb a tree and just lie on a branch listening to the birds sing and the squirrels chatter? When do preschoolers get to build forts out of cardboard boxes, castles out of sand, and tents out of old sheets and blankets? When do they have free time to just do what they want to do? When do they just get to be kids?

Perhaps, we parents have forgotten how to have fun too. Here are some suggestions to help put the child back into your little adult—and in yourself. Let these suggestions be springboards to stimulate your own creative juices in restoring the childlike spirit that Jesus said will be necessary for people to go to heaven.

- The next time it rains, take off your shoes and go wading together in the puddles.

- Take some string and pieces of bacon to a local creek and fish for crawdads together.

- Go outside and play hide-and-seek or kick-the-can with your kids and the neighbors' kids. You be "it" first.

- Have a birthday party for your child's pet. Bake a cake, and invite some of your child's friends to come to the party and bring their pets. Have special treats for the pets. Play party games that include the pets and act silly. Take pictures for your family scrapbook.

- Take some glass jars, one for each person, and punch holes in the tops. Pick an appropriate night, and go to the local park to catch fireflies. Then have a moonlight picnic in the park. Don't forget the mosquito spray!

- Turn your den into a movie theater for an afternoon. Cover the windows to create a dark theater atmosphere. Line up the chairs in rows. Rent funny movies that your children will enjoy. Beforehand, let your child make theater tickets and mail them to their friends. When they arrive, use a flashlight to lead the kids to their theater seats. Serve hot dogs, popcorn, and sodas.

- Go on a family flip-the-coin trip. Get in the car, and flip a coin. Heads you go right; tails you go left. At each corner, flip the coin and turn the direction the coin directs you. End up at a favorite ice cream parlor.

- Help your child put up a tent in the backyard and spend the night outdoors with your kids. Cook hot dogs on a campfire or grill. Read scary stories. Have favorite snacks. Play games. (And leave the cordless phone in the house!)

- Sponsor "Open Mic Night" on your patio or deck. Help your children send out announcements to their friends. Set up a karaoke system so the children can sing with a microphone and accompaniment tapes. Give each contestant a small prize for participating. Serve light refreshments.

- Take your kids and their friends to the circus when it comes to town. Clowns are good for the soul.

- Go on an all-day adventure in the woods. Pack your backpacks with lunch, energy snacks, and water. Take a book to read while you're resting. No radios or telephones! Don't make it a hard march, but a fun stroll through the woods to enjoy God's nature and each other.

- Take in all the local events that you can with your kids— parades, fireworks, outdoor community contests, etc. Watch your paper for family fun opportunities.

The name of the game is F-U-N. Kids need it desperately these days. And we adults need it too. It's one of the primary ingredients to sticking a family together and making unforgettable memories.

A Good Place to Start

When it comes to building a barrier between your family and evil, you need to spare no expense or time involvement. But where do you start evil-proofing your family? What steps can you take to protect them from the darkness?

My friend Dr. Paul Faulkner, president of Resources for Living and longtime popular marriage and family therapist, in his latest book titled *Raising Faithful Kids in a Fast-Paced World*, offers eight principles for successful families. He distilled these eight kernels of wisdom from intensive interviews with thirty successful families who have achieved excellence. His publisher has graciously granted me permission to include them here. I believe application of these eight good and godly principles to your family will erect a hedge of loving goodness and protection around them, lighting candles to drive away the evil darkness.

1. Parent on purpose—intentionally. Intentional is the opposite of *haphazard*. Intentionality means knowing what you want and aiming precisely to get it with all diligence. Parenting intentionally is based on a *focused mission* and clearly articulated *core values*. Three steps comprise intentional parenting: (1) set your sights on the target; (2) commit to hitting the bull's eye; and (3) never, ever give up.

2. Instill values—the foundation of the family. Successful families hold to and live out a clearly defined value system. These values are the framework, the measuring standard, for all they do and even for who they are. A proper value system does five important things: (1) blesses people, both inside and outside the family; (2) deals honestly with sin or wrongdoing; (3) lasts forever because it has been proven reliable through the years; (4) gives meaning and purpose to life; and (5) answers the "big questions" about life and death. In other words, a good value system gives value to the family.

3. Love them; adore them. Successful families have an obvious, effervescent, overflowing love for each child. They are extravagantly generous in their expressions of love for one another. The children are loved, and they know it. This warmth and love is shown in three distinct ways: (1) physical expressions of love, such as hugs and kisses, loving touches, a wink or a smile; (2) appreciation and encouragement; and (3) forgiveness. This love is not born into a child; it is learned from the parents and siblings. Love lavishly.

4. Lead from the foot of the table. Truly successful families are made up of servants, and the parents lead the family with a servant attitude. Creating a family success story constantly requires putting the needs of your children and your spouse above your own.

It requires that children serve their parents and each other willingly and lovingly. A servant heart is essential. Jesus is the perfect role model for leading from the foot of the table.

5. Give the gift of laughter. "On a scale of one to ten, humor is fifteen!" said one mom interviewed in Faulkner's book. Successful families laugh easily, and they laugh a lot. They learn to find humor in every situation, and they learn to laugh at themselves. Laughing and loving each other is a treasure never to be forgotten by children and parents alike.

6. Be transparent—communicate openly and honestly. When it comes to family communication, nothing should be taboo or swept under the table. There should be no family secrets from each other. Being vulnerable and *real* are vital to family health. Transparency, confession, and openness must begin with the parents, or it will rarely find its way to the children.

7. Hold them tight, then turn them loose. Great families encourage both roots and wings. They are made up of individuals who are both *networked*—recognizing that they occasionally want and need other family members to help them—and *autonomous*, or able to function self-sufficiently. Everyone supports everyone else, but each person is free and independent at the same time. Successful parents ground their children with roots—or principles to live by—and a strong, loving environment. Then they push the children to try their wings when the time is right—wings of aspiration and dreams to carry them into the future.

8. Learn to cope positively with tragedy and failure. Successful families are not victims, but victors. They place a high priority on overcoming the inevitable problems and obstacles that life throws in their paths. They persevere in spite of many negative, even desperate, circumstances. They learn to *reframe*, to make lemonade out of lemons.

The Letter

In the shabby basement of an old house in Atlanta, Georgia, lived a young widow and her little girl. During the Civil War, she had married a young Confederate soldier, against her Yankee father's will, and had moved with him south, to Atlanta. Her wealthy father, angry and hurt at what he considered to be her disloyalty, both to him and the North, told her never to come back again.

The soldier had died bravely during the war, and his death left his wife and child without any support. Alone in Atlanta, Margaret did washing, ironing, and other menial jobs that she could find to help her scrape by and feed little Anna. Their clothes became ragged, and they were both ill from sleeping in the damp, cold basement.

Anna loved to hear her mother's stories about her home in the North. She sat in her mother's lap and listened for hours to descriptions of the big, brick house in Boston, the sprawling shade trees, the beautiful flower gardens, and the wide grassy lawn. She loved to imagine the horses trotting across the meadow, the smell of bread baking in the kitchen, and the soft feel of the four-poster feather beds. Although Anna had never seen her mother's home, she thought it must be marvelous and secretly hoped that some day they would go there to live.

Margaret often sat looking wistfully up through the narrow basement windows at the blue sky, remembering her mama's smile, laughing with her two sisters, chasing her little brother, and sitting on her father's lap. She missed her family and home so much. But there was nothing she could do. She could never earn enough money to pay the train fare to Boston, no matter how hard she worked. And when she remembered her father's hurt, angry expression when she left, she knew there was little hope of ever seeing her family again.

One day the landlady of the house knocked on the basement door. Anna ran to answer, and the lady handed her a letter. Margaret knew immediately that the broadly scrawled handwriting on the envelope was her father's. With trembling fingers she pulled open the flap of the envelope. When she pulled out the single-sheet letter, two one-hundred dollar bills fell out on the floor. The letter had just three words: "Please come home."

Home. Our task is to make our homes a place where people will want to return. People like our mates, our children, our parents and grandparents. Home should be like a comforting fire on a winter day—the place where we all huddle together to stay warm, no matter what the weather is like outside. It should be a place of safety, love, and joy. And it's up to us to make it that way.

Everlasting Delight

After fifty-eight years of marriage, rearing four wonderful children, and now knowing the blessing of in-loves (our word for in-laws) and grandchildren, Helen and I highly recommend family life. We often tell young married couples, "We hope you will be as happy as we have been and are." There's nothing on earth more wonderful than a good marriage. We are partners, lovers, and best friends. All the joys have been doubled because we've been together. And when times have been hard, our troubles have been halved because we shared them.

It has been a tradition in our family for generations that the old hymn "Blest Be the Tie That Binds" be sung at each wedding. We thought, in our happiness, that we didn't need the singers to include the verse that says, "We share our mutual woes, our mutual burdens bear, and often for each other flows a sympathizing tear." But through the years we have found mutuality in sorrow a blessing beyond measure.

Above all, our faith in God has been our unifying force and has made all the difference for us. I can only hope that when we die that the same words can be said of our home and family as were written in the *20th Century Christian* magazine about my mother and father after her death:

Threescore years they loved each other devotedly. They made a great couple. The glance of the lover who rejoiced in his romantic achievement was still a bright gleam in her husband's eye after sixty years. Beauty of face, culture, wisdom, and bearing made loving her an everlasting delight. Their love was their driving force; they were the picture of domestic happiness. They had a home with an open door, an open hearth, and an open heart. Once a guest, always a friend. The young and the old went there. Spirits were lifted. Hearts were bright—optimism lived in every corner.

CHAPTER SEVEN

As Good
As Gold

secret

No. 7 – Manage your money; don't let it manage you. Spend wisely, save regularly, give generously—and pay your debts.

Dr. Ronald J. Sider

Professor, Eastern Baptist Theological Seminary;
President, Evangelicals for Social Action;
Author, *Rich Christians in an Age of Hunger*

A friend of mine has pioneered making tiny loans to very poor people in developing nations. His organization has discovered that on balance, each loan costs $500 and lifts a family of five by 50 percent within one year. At least one billion people today live without any education, health care, sanitation, or adequate food. Do you know how long it would take to lift the poorest one billion by 50 percent if we used just one percent of the annual income of all Christians today? Just one year!

Generous Christians could change our world. We know what to do. And we have the money. Do we have the generosity?

Whoever gives to others will get richer;
those who help others will themselves be helped.

Proverbs 11:25

The Power of Money Used for Good

A poor little girl named Hatti Wiatt once came to a small church in Philadelphia, Pennsylvania, and asked to attend their Sunday school. It was explained to Hatti that, unfortunately, because their building was so small there was just no room for her. So Hatti turned and sadly walked back to her tiny room where she lived alone.

Less than two years later, little Hatti became ill and died. Under her pillow was found a torn pocketbook with fifty-seven pennies in it. The pennies were wrapped in a scrap of paper on which Hatti had written, "To help build the little church bigger, so that more children can go to Sunday school." For two years Hatti had carefully saved her pennies for the cause that was nearest her heart.

When the minister of the little church was handed the ragged pocketbook and its fifty-seven pennies, he wept. Then he told Hatti's story to the church. The people were so moved that they began making donations to make little Hatti's dream come true. Newspapers told the story far and wide, too, and within five years those fifty-seven pennies had grown to $250,000—enough money in those days to build a large church building.

Today in Philadelphia stands a great church building that seats 3,300 people, a college with accommodations for more than 1,400 students, a Christian hospital, and a Sunday school facility so large that all who wish to learn may come. It's amazing what fifty-seven pennies used for good can accomplish.

Although we don't know how the two mites given by the widow in Luke 21 were used, or what they may have inspired later, we do know that great good came from their giving. Many Christians down through the ages have been humbled by her story and, as a result, become more generous in their own giving. The far-reaching results of her gentle generosity would be astronomical.

The results of Hatti's efforts remind me of a news story I heard a few years ago. The heading of the newspaper read "Pennies Block Traffic." The accompanying article explained that in Jessup, Maryland, a truck carrying 4.3 million pennies turned over on an entrance ramp to a highway, dumping copper-filled canvas sacks all over the highway. Traffic was tied up for several hours while police and guards cleared the road.

One penny alone would not have held up anything, but when 4.3 million pennies were brought together, they stopped traffic. Or, in Philadelphia they built a church, a college, a hospital, and a Sunday school.

Mrs. Blanche Ebert Seaver donated more than $161 million over a period of twenty years to Pepperdine University. But she lived frugally herself. Our liberal arts college is named Seaver College in honor of her late husband, Frank R. Seaver. Mrs. Seaver was an inspiration to me for many years in simplicity of living, generosity, and right priorities. She also wrote the music to this beautiful poem, which John Charles Thomas used to conclude each of his concerts on the well-known Firestone Hour:

Just for Today

Lord for tomorrow and its needs
    I do not pray;
Keep me, my God, from stain of sin,
    Just for today.

Now set a seal upon my lips,
    For this I pray;
Keep me from wrong or idle words,
    Just for today.

Let me be slow to do my will,
    Prompt to obey,
And keep me, guide me, use me, Lord,
    Just for today.

The Power of Money

Money, whether much or little, can be a powerful tool. When used for good, it can be powerfully good; when used for evil, it can be powerfully evil. The hand that holds it determines the kind of power it wields.

Ray O. Jones described money's dual personality well:

> Money talks, we have been told since childhood. Listen to the dollar speak: "You hold me in your hand and call me yours. Yet may I not as well call you mine? See how easily I rule you? To gain me, you would all but die. I am invaluable as rain, essential as water. Without me, men and institutions would die. Yet I do not hold the power of life for them; I am futile without the stamp of your desire. I go nowhere unless you send me. I keep strange company. For me, men mock, love, and scorn character. Yet, I am appointed to the service of saints, to give education to the growing mind and food to the starving bodies of the poor.

My power is terrific. Handle me carefully and wisely, lest you become my servant, rather than I yours."

Money has the power to build or destroy. It can encourage or discourage, help or hinder, energize or debilitate. Depending on how it's used, money can make or break a person or an organization.

Money is a subtle temptress who calls out to passersby like the siren of the sea who beckons weary sailors. Her voice is sweet and alluring, but her kiss is deadly. Falling in love with money is the first step toward disaster. And yet, she seems so innocent, so necessary, so appealing. She offers such comfort and joy. She promises contentment and respect. She holds out the luxuries of life in one hand, while she hides the loss of eternity behind her back in the other. "The love of money causes all kinds of evil. Some people have left the faith because they wanted to get more money, but they have caused themselves much sorrow" (1 Timothy 6:10).

Money can be like an unfaithful mate—here today and gone tomorrow. There's no more fickle lover than money. She flirts with you and then gives herself to someone else. She has no sense of loyalty or honor. She will love you and leave you, with no apologies and no explanations.

An author friend of mine keeps a constant reminder of money's fickleness by her computer where she works. In a picture frame she has mounted photocopies of two royalty checks she received for different publishing projects. At the top of the picture is the title, "The Tale of Two Books." Under the first check for $91,000 are the words "It was the best of times." Under the second check, in the amount of thirty-seven cents, are the words, "It was the worst of times." She says "The Tale of Two Books" keeps her humble and focused on what's really important in her life. It reminds her not to put her trust in money, which is here today and gone tomorrow, but in God, who never leaves her alone.

In these days of the greatest global prosperity in all of history, we need to be warned again of the dangers of money. The temptation to trust in our possessions is so subtle. As Lawrence Parkinson, the economist, once put it: "Expenses tend to rise to meet income and often to exceed it." It's like putting on extra pounds for those who tend to become too fat. Before we know it, we've become so used to luxuries that we think they're necessities, and so we must occupy ourselves even more with making money to satisfy our appetites for softer living.

Good Spending Patterns

But how can I live a simple, uncluttered life in the midst of all the pressures of a materialistic age? It's not easy. But either you manage your money or it will manage you. When you willingly become its slave, then it willingly becomes your master. And a cruel, demanding master it is. Once you are under its control, regaining mastery of money is extremely difficult.

John Templeton, who established the Templeton Prize for Progress in Religion and founded the Templeton Mutual Fund, says, "The thriftiness I was forced to learn became the foundation of my fortune." Working three jobs at a time, Templeton put himself through Yale University. And even with three outside jobs, he kept his grades in the top 1 percent of his class.

His scholastic success led to a Rhodes Scholarship for two years in England at Oxford University, where he earned a law degree. Then he and his wife took their first jobs, and they pledged to invest fifty cents of every dollar they earned in carefully researched common stocks. By detailed budgeting, they did just that for fifteen years.

Living on a strict budget wasn't easy, but they made it fun. Their friends enjoyed helping them find bargains. They never used a charge account or a credit card. And they never bought an automobile or a house except with cash. And through their years of prosperity, John and his wife discovered that it truly is "more blessed to give than to receive." For a number of years now, the winner of the annual Templeton Prize for Progress in Religion has received more than one million dollars, more than the amount given to recipients of the Nobel Prize.

So what are the secrets to putting money to work for good instead of evil? How can you keep your money from managing you? Here are a few suggestions to help us refocus our spending patterns for good.

MAKE YOUR FINANCES GOOD-CENTERED

Oseola McCarty, an eighty-eight-year-old woman who took in laundry in Hattiesburg, Mississippi, all her life, gave $150,000 to finance scholarships at the local college. Eager that others have chances that were never hers, she asked the bank to give her life savings, earned dollar by dollar, shirt by shirt, to the University of Southern Mississippi Foundation so that poor students could get an education. Living simply all her life, Oseola invested in a way that will create opportunities for others long after she is gone. And that's all she wanted to accomplish.

Her generosity touched so many people, though, that in the year following her gift Oseola found herself flying all over the country, appearing on network television, accepting humanitarian awards, and meeting famous people, including the president. Whoopi Goldberg knelt at her feet. Harvard gave her an honorary Doctor of Humane Letters. Her portrait now hangs in the administration building at the University of Southern Mississippi, the first portrait of a black person to be displayed there.

Why did all this happen? Simply because Oseola McCarty, a washerwoman, gave more than she took out of life. She reached out to help others. She shared her blessings. She placed "doing good" at the top of her financial priority list.

Plan your spending so that good has priority. Put aside money to do good things. Make the effort to financially support the good you see around you. Encourage others who are doing good. Make doing good your life's purpose and goal. Center your life, your thinking, and your spending on good. In other words, put God and good first.

W. L. Douglas, the now wealthy shoe manufacturer, was once unemployed for so long that he was down to his last dollar. Nevertheless, he put half of that dollar—fifty cents—in the collection basket of the church.

The next morning Douglas heard of a job in a neighboring town. The railroad fare to that town was one dollar. To all appearances it would have been wiser if he had kept that fifty cents. However, with the half-dollar remaining he bought a ticket and rode halfway to the desired place. He stepped from the train and began to walk to the town.

✧

You can never outgive God!

✧

Before he had gone one block, Douglas heard of a factory right in that town where they were hiring men. Within thirty minutes he had a job at a salary of five dollars more per week than he would have received had he gone on to the other town.

The point is, and it's been proven time and again, if we put God and good first, God will take care of the rest. But if we give him little or no place in our lives, we make him powerless to help us. Remember, you can never outgive God!

CHECK YOUR LIFE'S SPENDING DIRECTION EVERY MORNING

Will the spending you have planned for today contribute to the good of your life and that of others? Will your life be simpler or more complicated after you buy what you have planned to buy today? Are your finances on course with your life's good purpose? Will what you buy today bring you closer to God or force you farther away from him?

Helen's grandfather, F. L. Young, was the father of thirteen children. He worked as a traveling evangelist and was supported by church collections. Sometimes they were sufficient, but many times they were not. Still, they managed to live well because of his and his wife's frugality.

When Mr. Young's children asked to buy something, he would ask them, "Can you live without it until tomorrow?" If they said yes, then that's what they did.

We would probably all be amazed how many of the things we buy that we could do without until tomorrow . . . and the next day . . . and the day after that. Then we could give what we saved to the people who cannot do without what they need, such as food and shelter.

A young, mentally deficient boy named Joey had been saving his allowance for many months to buy a new bicycle he had seen in the department store window—a beautiful Red Flyer. Finally, he had saved enough money for the bike and ran downtown to buy it.

Just as he arrived at the store, he noticed a little girl on crutches standing by the show window of an adjacent store. She was looking at a small wheelchair, just her size. He could see that her right leg was in a brace, and he saw how tired she was from swinging herself along on the wooden crutches.

Smiling to himself, Joey went into the store and bought the wheelchair with his bicycle money and gave it to Jenny. Through the years, Jenny and Joey became best friends. Jenny was a very bright little girl, and she loved Joey for what he had done. She worked patiently with Joey and finally taught him how to read and write. Because of her unfailing friendship and help, Joey became a self-sufficient and respected man in the community. God surely blessed Joey for blessing Jenny.

CULTIVATE YOUR DESIRE TO HELP PEOPLE FINANCIALLY

Reach out to those who are less fortunate than you. Help people who can never repay you. Send someone some money anonymously in the mail. Learn to be truly generous to others—your family, your friends, and beyond.

When a sweet Christian lady named Terry found out about a family that needed financial help, she would buy several sacks of groceries. Then she and her children would drive to that family's neighborhood and park their car around the corner. The children would take the groceries and quietly set them on the front porch. Then they would ring the bell and run back to the car so they wouldn't be seen. After a few minutes, they would drive by the house to make certain the family had found the groceries. The people who had been helped never knew who had helped them . . . but God knew. And you can imagine the impact that simple good deed had on her children.

CURB YOUR APPETITE FOR LUXURIES

Evaluate your actual needs, not wants, and resist the urge to indulge yourself with expensive gadgets while millions have nothing to eat. Get radical! Choose some budgeted items that are dispensible, such as cable TV, expensive vacations, and eating out, and give the money you save each month to those in need.

One family of Christians illustrates this idea. They had ample money, but they *chose* to live very simply. The old farmhouse needed painting. Their clothes were always clean but plain. Their cars were in good repair but old.

The children in the family were extremely bright. One had a master's degree in education; the other had a doctorate in research science. Still, they *chose* a simple life with few luxuries . . . in all but one area. When it came to giving money to the church, they were lavish in their generosity. When other people needed help, they were the first to offer time, energy, and money. They quietly went about giving up their own luxuries to provide others' necessities.

This family did what all of us need to do. They determined what it actually cost them to live comfortably, then they gave the rest away to help others.

RESIST HIGH-PRESSURED SALES

Don't give in to the high-pressured advertising and sales presentations that appeal to your pride or your love of ease. One way to simplify your life is to set a household rule that you buy *nothing* over the telephone or at your door. Recognize that these two sales techniques capitalize on spur-of-the-moment decisions. They don't give you time to think through the sales pitch logically and calmly. Just learn to say, "I'm sorry, but I buy nothing over the telephone or at my door." (Obviously, Girl Scout cookies are the annual exception! After all, they are a well-thought-out, premeditated decision.)

Remember: things are not bargains at any price if you don't need them. Once you learn to spend cautiously, you will find that life can be lived lavishly. The confusion, discontentment, and self-centeredness will be gone. And life will be good . . . very good indeed.

WASTE NOT; WANT NOT

There is a marvelous economy of matter and energy in the natural world. Energy is transformed from one form to another with so little waste. The Bible teaches us that God places a premium upon the conservation of that which he has created. Jesus illustrated the principle of saving when he fed the five thousand people by having his disciples "gather up the fragments that remain, that nothing be lost." Both the Bible and common sense, based upon the observation of our material world, teach us that it's wrong to waste.

One of the encouraging signs of our times is the unprecedented emphasis on the conservation of our natural resources. We often see signs such as, "Water is precious; save it." And we see worldwide efforts to save our trees, wildlife, and natural resources.

Today the average American family is throwing away more food than the average primitive family in Asia or Africa has to eat. We waste more money foolishly than these poverty-stricken families would need to be housed and clothed. Can Christians condone and participate in this needless waste? Can a Christian family please God and spend money foolishly while millions of people need the bare necessities of life, to say nothing of their more urgent need of the Gospel of Christ?

Turn your waste into something good for others. Even your trash might sometimes financially help the cause of good! Some waste-management companies, for instance, pay for paper, plastic, and glass that can be recycled. Recycle yours! Then give the money to a worthy cause.

Learn to cook smaller portions. Most families don't do a good job of eating leftovers, and the leftovers end up in the garbage disposal. What a waste! Why not cook a little less and waste a little less?

Recycle your clothes. How many of us actually wear our clothes until they're worn out? Our closets are often bulging with clothes we never wear. And then we complain about not having enough closet space. Don't waste perfectly good clothes; give them to someone who needs them. Take them to a resale shop, and then give the money you earn to a needy family. Put them in someone's garage sale. Give them to the clothing room at the church. There is great need for used clothing in underdeveloped countries. Give them to an organization like Goodwill Industries or Union Rescue Mission. But don't just let them hang in your closet doing no good.

✧

Both the Bible and common sense teach us that it's wrong to waste.

✧

The Open Arms Home, Inc., a program for abused women and children in the Dallas-Fort Worth area, is an excellent example of how this can work. That program operates several resale shops called Second Glance stores. Christians donate their used clothing, furniture, and other resalable items to Second Glance. The store sells the items to the general public at bargain prices. Then the profit from the stores is used to help abused women and children. Now, that's turning your trash into triumph!

PAY YOUR DEBTS

Abused credit is choking the life out of Americans. Like an octopus, credit looks like something fun and interesting, until you get caught in its tentacles. Then you can't get away. Instead of your having credit, credit suddenly has you. And it squeezes and squeezes until the life goes out of you.

Pay off your debts! Being debt-free is one way to be truly free. The money you save on interest expense can be used to make additional money to help others. It is better to do without things, especially luxury items, than to buy them on credit.

A. A. Hyde, a millionaire manufacturer, said he began putting God first by tithing when he was one hundred thousand dollars in debt. Many people consider it dishonest to give God a tenth of their incomes while they are in debt to other people. Mr. Hyde said he agreed with that concept until one day it flashed upon his mind that God was his first creditor. He owed God more than he could ever pay. Then he began paying God first, and all the other creditors were eventually paid in full.

✧

"Pay everyone

. . . what you

owe."

✧

Sadly, in our society today, people often opt out of their debts. They take bankruptcy, protecting themselves while leaving their creditors high and dry. It's more common today than ever before in history. And yet, the apostle Paul said plainly in Romans 13:7, "Pay everyone, then, what you owe." We should consider our debts not only debts of money, but also debts of honor.

One of my good friends is now a prominent Southern businessman, but when the depression of the thirties struck, he was caught, along with thousands of others, in bad financial straits. The value of his holdings decreased overnight almost to the vanishing point. He found himself owing one bank over a hundred thousand dollars. Many men would have given up and taken the bankruptcy escape, but he felt a moral obligation to pay every dollar he owed.

Another bank in the city had his note for a comparatively small sum of some sixteen hundred dollars. The president of this bank called him in and handed him the note saying, "I know about your huge debt and, frankly, I don't think you can ever pay it out. Here is your note. We will not be bothering you about this debt."

He had the note. There was no legal obligation for him to pay it, but he knew that he still owed that money. He went to work and began to mend his fortune. His creditors wisely bore with him and trusted him to pay back at least part of his huge debt.

One day my friend walked into the office of the president of the bank that had canceled his note. He handed the banker his check for the full amount of sixteen hundred dollars, plus six percent interest from the date it had been borrowed. He had already paid off the large debt of more than a hundred thousand dollars, and now he wiped the slate clean by paying a moral obligation. He considered it a debt of honor.

J. Pierpont Morgan is reported to have said that he would rather have the oral word of an honest man than a thousand signatures of a crook. Pay your debts, and your light will shine brightly.

WILL YOUR MONEY TO DO GOOD

Society says, "What's mine is mine, and I can do with it as I please." And most people take this view of possessions. In Luke 12:18–21 the Bible tells the story of a rich man who believed society's philosophy. He said, "I will tear down my barns and build bigger ones, and there I will store all my grain and other goods. Then I can say to myself . . . rest, eat, drink, and enjoy life!" But God said to that man, "Foolish man! Tonight you will die. So who will get those things you have prepared for yourself?"

And Jesus concluded, "This is how it will be for those who store up things for themselves and are not rich toward God." Psalm 39:6 tells us, "All their work is for nothing; they collect things but don't know who will get them."

Like this rich man, most of us have not been taught to be good stewards of our possessions at death. But all our possessions are God's whether we live or die. And we have a responsibility to properly assign the use of God's assets, which he has put in our keeping, after we are gone.

Several years ago a prosperous young couple of our community was killed in an accident a few miles from their home. They owned a store and a number of valuable properties, but they had never made a will. The resultant legal difficulties in the disposition of their property caused me to think seriously enough to make my own will.

✧

"All their work is for nothing; they collect things but don't know who will get them."

✧

More than half of the people whose estates pass through the courts of our country have failed to make any kind of will. They simply leave their estates for disinterested court officials to distribute according to the letter of the law. I personally believe this is terribly irresponsible on the part of Christians.

If we truly believe James 1:17, which says "every perfect gift is from God," and Psalm 49:17, which says that a rich man "won't take anything to the grave," then we can surely see what a privilege and duty it is to direct that our gifts from God be used for him when we die.

It's important that we find knowledgeable Christian counselors to assist us, so that our assets are not wasted but continue to do good. My friend Mike O'Neal has helped hundreds of people in estate plannings to give generously to worthy causes without diminishing the amount left to their families. A well-planned will can be a Christian instrument for good to bless generations yet unborn.

Many years ago a friend left a million dollars to Pepperdine University when he died. We were elated at the prospect of building a new science building, which was urgently needed. Then we discovered that he had drawn his will in such a way that there were unac-

142

ceptable strings attached to the bequest. He had required that we confer an honorary doctor's degree upon a certain person. The university had to refuse the bequest on the grounds of integrity. We could not *sell* a degree, even for a million dollars. In spite of highest intentions, he didn't get competent legal advice, and the wording of the will left us no alternative but to turn down his bequest.

Sadly, thousands of Christians fail to plan carefully for the kingdom of God in their wills. And nothing out of their estates can go to the church, orphans' homes, Christian schools, or mission programs because they are not specified in their wills. If there is no will, the state is legally bound to simply divide your property among your relatives. It's a legal process called "intestate succession," which dictates how an estate is distributed. Unfortunately, relatives are not always considerate of the loved one's desire for Christian stewardship. In some cases the family will seek to carry out the wishes of the deceased, but such a family would appreciate all the more having the benefit of the deceased's expressed wishes.

Don't leave the disposition of God's assets to the sometimes godless courts. Take the time and energy required to be a good steward of his money, both in life and in death. Your earthly wealth should return to the Giver who gave it. It is your responsibility, your privilege, and it should be your joy to present your money and yourself as living sacrifices to God.

Test Yourself: Are You Wasteful?

God wants us to follow the example of his Son and refuse to "waste our substance." He wants us to live simply and use the profit of what we save to bless others throughout our lives. Why not do a self-check to find the areas in your life where you can improve?

1. Do you plan the use of your time so that you use the hours for work, worship, rest, and recreation properly?

2. Do you budget your income so that you live within your means?

3. Do you practice thrift in buying what you actually need, not just what someone sells you?

4. Do you waste food by cooking more than is needed or ordering more at a restaurant than you can eat?

5. Do you waste electricity by leaving the lights on all over the house when no one needs them? Do you waste water or gas?

6. Do you waste money by buying more clothes than you actually need? Are your closets filled with good clothes that some less fortunate person needs to keep warm?

7. Are you teaching your children to be wasteful by being wasteful in front of them?

8. List three things you can do to reduce the waste in your life and help others by what you save.

CHAPTER EIGHT

Good News, Bad News

secret

No. 8 – "Test everything. Keep what is good, and stay away from everything that is evil."

—1 Thessalonians 5:21–22

Dr. William S. Banowsky

Former President and CEO,
Gaylord Broadcasting Corporation

In 1835, Sören Kierkegaard predicted deification of
the free press as democracy's downfall. Today, as
our Supreme Court debates delivery in cyberspace
of every conceivable human perversion, the
Kierkegaardian nightmare haunts the planet.
Beleaguered families are under siege! What a
dilemma: Survival demands tougher censorship,
but the free society can never abandon its free
press. Since we can't live without it, we must find
a better way to live with it. Norvel Young's call to
fight evil with the Good News is that better way.

Good news makes you feel better.
Your happiness will show in your eyes.

Proverbs 15:30

The Power of Good in the Media

Oone cold evening I came in off our balcony that overlooks the Pacific Ocean. I clicked on the television for the evening news. To my delight, the news commentator was telling a heartwarming story—some *good* news for a change.

Tom Nichter had seventy-five cents in his pocket that Thursday evening in February—all that stood between his family and hunger. They were homeless, living in their old car. He and his wife, Pauline, had been jobless for months because of cutbacks at their work. Bills were mounting mercilessly.

Pauline remembered, "We were at the lowest point in our lives that evening. We were out of work, out of money, and had no place to live. We were pretty much out of hope too."

Tom and Pauline's eleven-year-old son, Jason, wanted to go to the mall just to look around. So they went. Pauline waited while

Jason ran up and down the aisles of the toy store pointing out toys and games to his dad. She was looking around idly when she saw a gray leather folder, like a big wallet, on top of a stack of games. She took another look and noticed there seemed to be money inside. She remembered thinking, *It must be play money*, as she picked up the wallet. She was shocked to see that the money was *real* . . . and there was a lot of it.

Pauline showed Tom and Jason the wallet. "Could this be meant for us?" She and Tom thought briefly of all the ways they could put that money to use. It appeared to be two or three hundred dollars— a small fortune to them. They quickly decided, though, that the money was not theirs, and they didn't want to set a bad example for Jason. So, they closed the wallet and looked for a security guard.

When they couldn't find a guard, they drove several miles, using up their precious gasoline, to take the wallet to the Buena Park police station. When they entered, Sergeant Terry Branum was talking to Jay Schermerhorn, a KNBC-TV cameraman who was at the station. Pauline placed the wallet on the counter in front of Sergeant Branum and said, "We found this at the mall. We don't even really know what's in it."

Sergeant Branum was surprised to find credit cards, a passport, a fifteen-hundred-dollar plane ticket, and $2,394 in cash. Tom was amazed that it was so much money. The sergeant asked Tom to tell him the story. Slowly, Tom described their situation and how they had come to find the wallet. He related how he had been looking for a steady job for over two years. Then, a year ago, Pauline's division of her company was closed too. Despite an excellent work record, she had been unable to find employment since.

Schermerhorn stood by, taking in the station drama. He suggested to Sergeant Branum that they do an interview when the wallet owner was found. The officer called the mall and was told that the owner had just come in to report the lost wallet.

In twenty minutes, a relieved tourist reclaimed his wallet and its contents as the TV camera recorded the scene. The man thanked the Nichters profusely, but he offered no reward. Later that night the

Nichters were out eating hamburgers (on three dollars given to them by Sergeant Branum) while we watched their story on the evening news.

A Little Good News

The next morning reporter Erin Kelly of the *Orange County Register* called the police station to find out if anything newsworthy had happened. Sergeant Branum told her about the Nichters.

"That's a *great* story!" said Kelly excitedly. "The whole paper is just dead bodies today, and I'd love to print some *good* news."

The Nichters' story of honesty and goodness made page one. It was also picked up by the wire services and spread to media all over the U.S. and abroad. Theirs was the "good deed heard 'round the world." The police station was soon overwhelmed with people calling who wanted to help the Nichters. Calls came in from as far away as Toronto, London, and Istanbul. One person walked into the police station and asked how much money had been in the wallet. When Sergeant Branum told him, he wrote a check for $2,400, handed it to the officer and said, "They deserve at least that."

By the next Monday, mail was pouring into the police station from everywhere. Some days it took six people eight full hours just to open the envelopes. Inside were good wishes, prayers, and donations from fifty cents to hundreds of dollars. Everyone wanted to help the Nichters get back on their feet and reward their good deed.

Our local businesses took up collections and dropped off boxes filled with canned goods, paper products, and toiletries. The family received a bed for Jason, airline tickets to anywhere they wanted to go in the U.S., and many other things they needed so badly. A Realtor even offered them six months' free rent in an apartment she owned in Garden Grove. And job offers came for both Tom and Pauline from all over.

The Nichters were amazed at the response to their act and absolutely overwhelmed by the goodness of people. "After all," said Tom, "we didn't do anything special. We only did the *right* thing."

In reality, they did so much more with their simple act of honesty and goodness. For a society lost in the blackness of constant murders, robberies, and mayhem, the Nichters lit a candle in the darkness. Their story reminded other people that good dispels evil, and those people responded by lighting their own candles of goodness in return.

Media Out of Focus

A simple act of goodness in a shopping mall became international news in less than twenty-four hours. That's media power! And that's using the media for good purposes.

In our electronic multimedia society, it's practically impossible to be uninformed. If you don't take the time to sit down and watch the news on television, you probably hear it blaring at you from the radio, see it in the papers and magazines, or it pops up on your own personal computer screen via the Internet. Almost nothing on earth is done in secret anymore.

Where were you when former president John F. Kennedy was shot? Almost everyone alive when it happened can tell you exactly where they were when they heard or saw the dramatic news report. It was shocking, world-shattering news that flew around the globe in an electronic minute. Suddenly, the whole world had heard the bad news.

Then, day by day, the horrific story unfolded on television, radio, and the newswires, in newspapers, magazines, and tabloids, and anywhere else print or the airwaves would allow. It was a media field day that lasted for weeks. Even today, every year on the anniversary of Kennedy's death, we are reminded by the media of what happened. The bad news lingers.

And can any of us forget the blow-by-blow account of Desert Storm that invaded our living rooms via television for days on end? Those live accounts riveted our attention. Looking at Saddam Hussein in the newspaper is one thing, but having him for breakfast, lunch, and dinner day after day was much more than most of us wanted.

Bad news prevails in the media. Why? Because disaster, murder, war, and tyranny are considered *newsworthy*. Bad news attracts attention to itself. It grabs the spotlight and dances its grotesque way into our purview. It cannot be ignored. These stories and events demand to be told because of their dramatic impact on people. They are powerful and aggressive, in a negative way, and act as magnets to reporters and newshounds. People who have the proverbial "nose for the news" sniff out bad news like a hound dog sniffing out a skunk.

Songwriter and singer, Anne Murray, expressed my feelings, though, when she sang the song, "I Sure Could Use a Little Good News Today." I'd like to hear about more people like the Nichters. I'd like to see more stories about Mother Teresa and fewer reports on terrorists. I'd like to hear about an honest politician once in a while or a cost-saving government program or a dog that *saved* a child's life rather than viciously attacking one. Wouldn't that be refreshing? Give me an hour's worth of good news, and I'm energized. It's encouraging and inspiring. It's motivating.

✧

Media's job is to report the news; our job is to make the news with goodness.

✧

Help Media Refocus

What we need to do is refocus media's attention away from evil and toward good. In order to do that, we have to report goodness in action, as well as making sure that our own lights are shining, so that media has dramatically good people and events to tell the world. We need to constantly look for the good, the inspiring, and the noble and take the time to share those stories with the media.

Let's not be so passive and anemic that media overlooks our good actions and events. Media's job is to *report* the news; our job is to *make* the news with goodness and to point out the goodness of others. It does no good just to condemn the reporters; we have to give them something else to report. Good news is news, and when they know about it, media will report it. It's encouraging to see, for instance, *Time* magazine's weekly column called "Local Heroes" and a new television program to report good news called *What's Right with L.A.*

A minister in Wyoming recently began writing scripts for television. One of his projects was to rewrite a Dennis Weaver movie to eliminate the bad language. The producers told him, "Christians throw stones at us, but they don't throw scripts at us."

A minister friend of mine named Furman Kearley continued this thought by saying, "We have not been willing to spend enough money and support good Christian talent. We have failed to see the power of dramatic productions to proclaim the powerful story of Christ and Christianity." Furman has given us five ways to impact the media for good on an ongoing basis:

1. Encourage talented Christian people to write television and movie scripts, both for the secular media and to be produced by Christians.

2. Encourage talented singers and composers, especially young people, to write and perform good songs.

3. Write and support those who write books of good quality.

4. Produce entertaining television programming that exalts Christian values. Television writer/director/producer Michael Landon, over a period of more than thirty years, was able to write and produce many high-level programs with good morals and values.

5. Pray and work to eliminate pornography and to elevate television, movies, videos, and books.

Granted, making the news with goodness sounds like role reversal to Christians who have worked so hard through the years to stay out of the news, because the news was almost always bad. And yet, if the news rarely *reports* goodness, even if goodness is happening quietly all around us, the reading/listening public may logically conclude that evil predominates life. Children and teens who are exposed to primarily negative news will likely assume that the world is negative and that they have to be negative, too, in order to fit in. Peer pressure is a powerful force.

And isn't that exactly what's happened? Young people take guns to school, do drugs, commit suicide, participate in drive-by shootings, and join gangs, primarily because they think everybody is doing it and that there is really no alternative for them. They don't hear about good as an alternate choice, so how can they make the choice? In fact, media plays up their evil in the public eye so much that they become infamous—famous in a negative way—which to them is better than being a good nobody. In a perverted kind of way, media unintentionally builds evil heroes simply by consistently reporting the *dark news* and rarely reporting the *light news.*

We are called to take the light to a world where wrong seems right. If we take our calling seriously, we will be active in our role as the light of the world. We will take the light to the world every day of our lives. And the public media—both electronic and print—is the fastest, most efficient way to do it.

Helping Media Notice Good News

We have to help media *notice* the good that's being done around the world. If they don't know about it, they can't report it. Here are some practical, doable ways to get the print media to notice goodness in action.

WRITE LETTERS TO THE EDITOR

Most local newspapers and magazines have a "Letters to the Editor" section in which they invite their readers' letters expressing personal opinions. You don't have to be a brilliant journalist to write a simple letter pointing out some good news event in your community. This is an open forum, which is most normally dominated by complainers. Most editors are pleased to receive a positive, upbeat letter they can run to counterbalance all the negative ones they get.

SEND CHEERS AND JEERS

A popular concept that has made its way into many magazines and papers is the "Cheers and Jeers" columns. You can *write* a cheer for something good and worthwhile and submit it to the publication. Or, you can write a jeer to point out something bad and harmful.

The great thing about cheers and jeers is its ability to praise good and condemn evil. Make yourself a note and put it by your computer or desk to write a cheer as often as feasible. (If you submit them too often, the editor will probably not be able to print them all.) Be selective in the ones you submit to ensure that they are truly worth the cheer and not just filler material.

SUBMIT GOOD-NEWS ARTICLES AND FEATURES

Newspaper editors are some of the most harried people alive. They are required to come up with enough newsworthy material every day to fill their section of the paper. Some days that's easy; some days it's hard.

These editors will be happy to receive *quality* news articles or tips about *real* news stories that they can cover. And you can become a reliable source of stories for them by following these professional guidelines:

1. Submit only solid, newsworthy articles or ideas.
An ordinary baby shower in the fellowship room of your church will not draw media attention (unless you're in a very small town). But an unusual, dramatic event will.

For instance, a large church in Texas recently took to heart the Bible teaching to honor those in government (1 Timothy 2:1–2). The church had a special assembly honoring the attorneys, judges, and justices of their city, county, and state. These civil servants were formally invited to attend the service in their honor, and about eighty members of the bar and judiciary came, including the state's chief justice.

Prior to the actual event, the minister planning the assembly notified the local newspapers and media of the potential news story. Because the event was unusual and involved prominent people in the community and state, the media came to cover the service. The next day's news articles drew positive attention to Christ, the church, and its ongoing activities.

If you consistently submit truly newsworthy story ideas to your editors, before long you may find *them calling you* to see what's happening. And don't confine the story ideas that you submit to those that will benefit you or your organization either. Give your editors *any* newsworthy story you come across. That way, editors won't feel as if you're simply using them to feather your own nest. If you help them, then they can legitimately help you from time to time.

2. Make friends with the media. Get to know some of the editors, radio newspeople, television news personalities, and others who report the news. Don't be timid. They're just people like you, doing their jobs. Try to be helpful when you can by giving them tips and ideas. Invite them to lunch to get acquainted. Drop them a note praising a feature article that carried their byline. Ask them for advice about how you can properly interact with them to get some good news on the air and in print. In other words, build a sincere relationship with them.

In our society, networking is the name of the game. Relationships rule! You can't expect to hide in your home or office and gain anyone's attention, much less media's. They have to know who you are and that you're reliable and reportable. Just make friends with them. After all, a friend is more likely to report your story accurately and positively than someone who doesn't know you.

3. Use the right format. When you submit a prewritten article or press release to the media, use the accepted, professional format. Go to your public library and look it up. Or, call the newspaper or magazine you wish to make submissions to and ask for their writer's guidelines. In other words, do your homework.

The closer you can prepare your submission to the style and format the editor can use, the better chance you have of getting your material accepted for publication. Submit it in a professional way, which will entice them to print it.

A friend of mine used to prepare press releases about Campaigns for Christ and submit them to newspapers around the country. She had done her homework and learned to prepare those releases in the preferred journalistic style of most papers. As a result, her success rate in getting those articles published was over 90 percent.

The bottom line is this: Make it easy for them to say yes to the material you send them. Remove all the roadblocks and frustrations by using proper grammar, correct punctuation, acceptable capitalization, and professional journalistic style. Answer all their content questions. Provide all the sources for quotes you use. Do all the work for them. Then it becomes difficult for them to refuse your work. A great resource is *The Chicago Manual of Style*, which is considered the top authority for putting material into publishable form.

USE PUBLIC-SERVICE ANNOUNCEMENTS

By law, radio stations are required to provide the general public with a certain amount of time for Public-Service Announcements (PSAs). These announcements inform the public about important and worthwhile upcoming events. Anyone can submit a PSA to a radio station, either in writing or as a professionally prepared recording. This is a perfect place to focus media's attention on good news by submitting PSAs that announce good public events.

Most PSAs are limited to one minute or less. Many stations limit them to only thirty seconds. Our task is to professionally prepare quality PSAs based on truly newsworthy ideas in the accepted format.

Now, you can often submit your PSAs in writing via e-mail over the Internet. You don't even have to leave your home or office to impact the media for good.

One church chorus I know uses PSAs to invite the public to their programs and concerts. They have found that their attendance increases sharply when the PSAs are run compared to when no PSAs are used. Each time the PSA runs on the air people hear "a little good news today."

Using Technology to God's Advantage

The technological advances made in the field of communication in the last few years are astounding! Instead of focusing on the misuse of this new technology, let's light our candles and use them for His good. The extent of satellite technology, for example, is amazing, and we should use it to send Good News into every part of the world. For instance, in April 1996, one worldwide Christian television series was interpreted into more than forty-five languages and seen in more than two hundred countries simultaneously via satellite. It's a modern-day version of what happened at Pentecost. What a marvelous way to use the media and modern technology to benefit the cause of Christ.

CYBERCRIME VERSUS CYBERSALVATION

We've all heard about the pitfalls of the Internet and, yet, the Internet, like any other tool, can be used for good or for evil.

In January 1997, for instance, a woman in Maryland was murdered by a man she had chanced to meet and converse with on the Internet. That's certainly using the Internet for evil.

However, the Maryland police solved the murder by using special software to retrieve deleted e-mail messages from the victim's computer, which had been sent by the murderer. The murderer, in effect, left his cyber-fingerprints on the victim's hard drive. So, the police used the Internet in a good way to bring justice to the victim's killer. It's not the Internet that's good or evil; it's those who use it.

I'm thrilled to hear from Christians all over the world who are building Websites and setting up electronic shopping malls that feature only top-quality Christian materials. Most Christian schools and universities are now on-line. Churches are setting up home pages and putting out the Good News on the web. From my personal computer I can even send unlimited e-mail messages of encouragement to missionaries and friends internationally for a nominal monthly fee.

Every Christian who has a phone line and a computer can be in the multimedia Good News business. It's one of the most important developments for Christianity and spreading the gospel since the printing press. Think about all the wonderful things people can do right from their home keyboards:

- People can conduct personal Bible studies in private electronic "chat" rooms with interested students from all over the world.

- Christian counselors can offer comfort and help to those who are suffering emotional pain when those people might be embarrassed to go to a counselor in person.

- Condolence and congratulatory messages can be transmitted instantly.

- Ministers can give advice and answer biblical questions from their members without either of them having to make trips out into the weather or traffic.

- Christian products and services can be made available worldwide at a fraction of the marketing and advertising cost previously required, even to remote areas where travel is difficult.

- Families can stay in touch with each other more easily and more often, probably with no long distance or mail charges.

- Homebound people can tune in to hear Christian singers and messages from ministers right on their computers at home. Physically limited people will no longer be deprived of Christian services, products, and assistance.

- More Christian parents can now work at home effectively and take care of their children themselves, rather than having to leave them with others during their formative years.

And the list can go on for pages. It is, for me, a most exciting innovation. Our challenge is to learn how to use the Internet and World Wide Web to the best advantage for the Gospel. The seemingly impossible task that Jesus gave his disciples to "Go and make followers of all the people in the world" (Matthew 28:19) has become entirely possible! Every day more and more people go on-line, and each new connection is an electronic door of opportunity for the Lord and his Good News.

DON'T BE SCARED OF A LITTLE MOUSE

I often hear older Christians say the electronic age is frightening to them and that they can't understand it. I am older than some others, but I can still learn what I set my mind to, and so can most of my friends. We must be willing to make the effort to understand the electronic age. The mind must be challenged, as well as the body, if we are to stay alive as long as we live. Granted, we didn't grow up doing math by clicking a mouse, but when you think of the hundreds of amazing inventions we've had to learn to use in our lifetimes, computers are just the next step.

Most of us learned to type on an old manual typewriter. Then we learned to use an electric typewriter. The computer is just the next generation. Truthfully, we often make computers more mystical than they really are. And mastering them is just a matter of time and effort.

159

Christians surfing the Web and chatting about their faith is one way to light the world. Experienced Christians have so much knowledge and wisdom to offer seekers who are browsing the Net looking for hope and help. Retired Christians often have more time to reach out an electronic hand to others and gently draw them to the grace of God. And they can do it from the comfort of their homes.

I think the electronic age is made to order for older Christians. It's not physically demanding to work a computer; you can turn it off anytime you choose. It keeps you mentally alert and active. Surfing the Internet and stopping off in a "chat" room to converse with other people who share your particular interests provides companionship and entertainment, and you can shop for whatever you need without having to leave the house.

Taking on Television

"This season," said *US News and World Report* in late 1996, "it's sex, not violence, that obsesses the writers of prime-time shows." In what *Time* called an "alarming trend," sexual references on prime-time programs are growing more explicit, more frequent and more irresponsible. In only one year, from 1994 to 1995, the sex-related incidents on prime-time shows increased by 30 percent.

Once a haven for family-oriented programs, the early evening hours have become, in the words of the *Wall Street Journal,* "a hotbed of sex and other spicy fare." Peter Jacobson, the producer of "The Nanny" on CBS, made this telling statement: "I believe it's okay to run anything on television any time."

The damage being done to children and families is disastrous! For example, when researchers offered four- and five-year-olds the choice between giving up television or their fathers, *one third* opted to give up Daddy. And, in one survey, teenagers themselves said that television is the single greatest source of pressure to become sexually involved.

The real crime of prime time goes beyond sex, though, to television's underlying message. Former Secretary of Education Bill

Bennett says this: "The philosophy being so powerfully promulgated is basically this: The [greatest good] of life is self-indulgence and instant gratification; the good life is synonymous with license and freedom from all inhibitions; other people are to be used as a means to an end; and self-fulfillment is achieved by breaking rules."

Aren't the talk shows outlandish (with very few exceptions)? Every lurid form of humanity parades across the television screen, exposing the most despicable lifestyles imaginable. The more twisted the situation, the better the hosts seem to like it.

And while Bill Bennett and other leaders have begun to act, most Americans are still sitting on the sidelines being passively good, but doing nothing to change the evil that comes into their very own living rooms.

A Gallup poll showed that fewer than 2 percent of adults have complained to a television station. The networks claim that "almost no" viewers have complained about adult fare during the early evening hour.

Why do so few of us complain? The most common reasons offered by those who participated in a mail survey by *Positive Living* magazine were "I didn't think it would do any good" and "I didn't know how." What can one person do about it anyway? You can't take on the networks and win, can you?

When Phil Donahue, "The King of TV Talk Shows," left the air, many people gave much of the credit to *one man:* Richard Neill. He's become known as "the dentist who dethroned Donahue." By long-term diligent and determined efforts, he chipped away at Donahue's throne, by organizing letter-writing campaigns to the program sponsors, appealing to senators and representatives, and finally even appearing on the Donahue show himself, at Donahue's invitation.

Here's how one prominent advertiser responded to Dr. Neill's letter: "We are stopping all advertising support of *The Donahue Show.* Dr. Neill, we have a strong desire to ensure that our brands are advertised on quality television programming, and we share your concern for children's viewing. We thank you for your efforts to encourage better television."

And here's another one from the CEO of John Paul Mitchell Systems: "Dr. Neill, I have put in a recommendation that we withdraw our advertising from shows described in your letter. I agree, we've got to clean up America."

In January 1996, after hundreds of advertisers and scores of stations, including those in New York and San Francisco, had dropped his show, Phil Donahue announced that he was leaving the show permanently. His last show was taped in May 1996. The facts show that Dr. Richard Neill played a significant role in Donahue's departure from television.

Is Richard Neill an extraordinary man? Not really. He's a dentist. He's a husband. He's a dad who got tired of taking it from television and decided to take television on. He did it, and he won. Yes, you can take on the networks and win. The consumer is king; we just aren't exercising our power.

You may wish to read Neill's own telling of the incident in *Taking on Donahue and TV Morality*, as described in the Resources and Opportunities for Good appendix. We have also provided a list of the top-ten television advertisers and their addresses, so that you can help clean up television. You may not be able to invest a year of your life in a television cleanup campaign like Dr. Neill—of course, the more hours you invest, the more impact you will probably have—but even one hour will help.

You can do what one family did to protect themselves from the harmful effects of some television programs—they *adopted their television*. To defend your own family, decide that any program that comes into your home has to be as family-friendly as anyone who lives there. Hold an adoption ceremony for your television. Give the set a name, like "Mike." Make the children and adults understand that Mike will be held to the same standards as everyone else in the house. If he starts bringing stories, pictures, or language into the house that might harm other family members, Mike must take a "time out." He will be turned off for a while.

Whenever your adopted child misbehaves, immediately change the channel or turn him off. Use those occasions to tell your kids,

"Those values and behaviors are not ours because they are harmful." And explain why.

By All Means, Do It

Whether you're a young computer Web master whizzing around the electronic universe or a retired person who prefers to read your newspaper quietly over a cup of coffee, there is a way for you to influence the media for good. Letters to the editor or to television sponsors can be e-mailed or handwritten. Good news stories can be written, phoned in, faxed, or transferred over the Internet to your local paper. No matter *how* you choose to do it, by all means and any means, *do it!*

Several years ago, General Electric's advanced technology laboratory in Schenectady, New York, designed an invention they called the Pedipulator. It was a seventeen-foot-high robot skeleton. A man could stand inside the Pedipulator's "skull" and manipulate the machine through his own arm and leg movements. The Pedipulator amplified the normal power of the man's limbs many times over, enabling the man to perform superhuman feats.

Imagine a man stepping over parked cars, uprooting a tree, carrying a telephone pole up a cliff by himself, or racing through an impassable swamp. A man in the Pedipulator could do all those things and more.

The developers were excited. One said, "It's extremely difficult to teach a robot to do things. But this joins man and machine. Now we have man's brain and nervous system joined to the machine's great strength." Together they could be almost invincible.

The Pedipulator never actually came to be, due to technical difficulties. But don't we have something very similar in the media? The amazing electronic news media around the world can take ordinary people who perform random acts of kindness and turn them into superheroes, like the Nichters. It can take a little local athletic event and transform it into an international festival called the Olympics.

And by combining our voices and minds with media's power, we can take the simple Good News of Jesus to a spiritually destitute world. If you listen very carefully, perhaps you can hear, as I often do, the hearts of the lonely and hopeless people around the world crying to us softly, "We sure could use a little Good News today."

CHAPTER NINE

The Good-Neighbor Policy

secret

No. 9 – Love your next door neighbor
as well as the one who lives around
the world, through compassionate,
proactive deeds of service.

Robert A. Seiple

President, World Vision

Lots of people desire to be good. Greatness, however, is defined as aggressive goodness. And the great should never be held hostage to that which is merely good. Tolerance in community affairs, for example, is touted by almost everyone. But why should we simply tolerate people when it is within our sphere of choices to love them? Aggressive goodness calls us to the higher value.

Good people bless and build up their city.

Proverbs 11:11

The Power of Good in the Community

1969. Pepperdine College, then located on the edge of the Watts District of Los Angeles, had weathered the stormy racial riots of 1965 without being devastated. But those turbulent days showed us the wisdom of setting up a supplemental campus. We were searching for the right property and excited about our dreams and plans for expansion.

Late one afternoon I was walking the three blocks from my office in the administration building to the president's home on campus, when I saw a group of people in front of Marilyn Hall—the girls' dormitory. I remember that the dorm seemed larger to me than usual that day as I walked toward it. Suddenly my thoughts were interrupted.

Shouting! A woman screaming. People pointing and running. As I hurried to investigate, the crowd, some of whom were Pepperdine students, parted. That's when I saw him.

167

Larry Kimmons, a neighborhood African-American high school boy was lying on the ground . . . dying. Blood was all over and around him. The woman screaming was Larry's mother. My heart went out to her, and then it jumped into my throat as I thought about the possible implications.

The arrival of an ambulance and police cars with their sirens blaring and the growing, racially charged crowd made it difficult to sort out exactly what had happened. Eventually, though, it became clear, both to me and the police.

Pepperdine had always tried to be a good neighbor to the people who lived adjacent and near our campus. There was a backlog of goodwill between the college and our neighbors. For instance, we allowed neighborhood youth to play in our gymnasium regularly. It was a good way to help keep them off the dangerous streets and in a safer environment. That evening Larry and a friend had come on campus to play basketball in the gym but were told that the gym had to be closed for another function and they wouldn't be able to play that night.

Frustrated that they were not able to use the gym, Larry and his friend had come back on campus two more times to insist that they be allowed to play. Our campus chief of security, Charles Lane, had continued to refuse entrance to them that night, out of necessity.

Finally, becoming angry, Larry had attacked Mr. Lane, trying to take away his shotgun and force his way into the gym. Tragically, the gun had accidentally discharged during the struggle, critically wounding Larry.

As soon as I could, I went home and called Bill Banowsky, the university president. I told him what had happened and asked him to come back to campus. He came immediately, and we went directly to the Kimmons' home to express our distress and sympathy. We went out of Christian concern and against the advice of the local police. We felt we could do no less, in spite of the peril we might face in the tension-taut neighborhood.

By this time, television and radio news were reporting Larry's death. Police cars were assembling *en masse* on our campus in anticipation of possible racial retaliation. And even though we had worked hard through the years to build good relationships with our community, this incident added to the general jitters of the social climate.

We received threats from various callers, the media was all over us, and a volatile group of students issued demands to us. In a called meeting of faculty, they voted to accede to all demands from the students in order to show our sensitivity and true concern for the situation.

Bill and I were up all night, talking with the Kimmons family and negotiating with the students and neighbors, just trying to keep an emotional lid on things. Fortunately, the mutual respect and cooperation Pepperdine had amassed over thirty years with the surrounding community of people made it possible for us to get through the disaster without further complications. Being a good neighbor had truly paid off.

Love Your Neighbor

When Jesus was asked what was the greatest commandment of all, he said, "Love the Lord your God. Love him with all your heart, all your soul, all your mind, and all your strength." Then he said, "The second command is this: 'Love your neighbor as you love yourself'" (Mark 12:30–31).

Of all the commandments given by God, only one outranks loving our neighbors, and that's loving God himself. And if we're not loving our neighbors, who are made in the image of God, we're not really loving God either. As the old cartoon character, Hambone, used to say it: "There ain't no use trying to talk to God when you ain't speakin' to your neighbor."

"And who is my neighbor?" asked the teacher of the law.

✧

"There ain't no use trying to talk to God when you ain't speakin' to your neighbor."

✧

169

Then Jesus told him the parable of the Good Samaritan (Luke 10:30–37). And he concluded by asking the teacher of the law, "Which one of these three men"—the priest, the Levite, or the Samaritan—"do you think was a neighbor to the man who was attacked by the robbers?"

The teacher of the law answered, "The one who showed him mercy."

And Jesus said to him, "Then go and do what he did!"

> ✦
>
> Neighbors are everywhere you look. They are everybody you meet everywhere you go.
>
> ✦

In other words, your neighbor is the person in the ditch. Your neighbor is the one who's in trouble, in pain, or in peril. Your neighbor is your enemy, your friend, or someone you don't even know. He's the poor, the lonely, the sick. He's the jobless and the joyless. He's the homeless, the hopeless, and the helpless. He's the shut-in and the shut-out. He's the hungry and the hefty. He's one person one day and someone else the next. *Your* neighbor is anyone who needs *your* help.

Perhaps your neighbor is the single mom across the street whose baby-sitter quit today. It might be an elderly lady next door whose fence is falling down because she can't repair it herself. Maybe it's the little boy on your block whose daddy recently deserted him. Or it could be the teenager in your Sunday school class who's fighting to stay off drugs.

In truth, neighbors are everywhere you look. They are everybody you meet everywhere you go. And our job, as Christians, is to love them as much as we love ourselves, care for them as we would care for ourselves, protect them as we protect ourselves, help them, teach them, save them.

What Does a Community Look Like?

An ordinary community or city is made up of a variety of people. The *Merrill Lynch Newsletter* suggests that if we could shrink the earth's population to a village of precisely one hundred people, with all existing human ratios remaining the same, its demographics would look like this:

- There would be 57 Asians; 21 Europeans; 14 from the Western Hemisphere (North, Central, and South America); and 8 Africans.
- 51 would be female; 49 would be male.
- 70 would be nonwhite; 30 white.
- 70 would claim to be non-Christian; 30 would claim to be Christian.
- 50 percent of the entire world's wealth would be in the hands of only 6 people, and all 6 would be citizens of the United States.
- 80 would live in substandard housing.
- 70 would be unable to read.
- 50 would suffer from malnutrition.
- 1 would be near death; 1 would be near birth.
- Only 1 would have a college education.

And did you know that . . .

- the world's largest cities are growing at a rate of more than one million inhabitants per week?

- according to current projections, by the year 2000 there will be twenty-six cities in the world with a population of 10 million or more each?

- three of the ten largest cities in the world are located in South America? They are São Paulo and Rio de Janeiro, Brazil; and Buenos Aires, Argentina. Between them, these three cities have a population exceeding forty million.

These astounding statistics came from the *Urban Missions Newsletter* in Westminster, and they point up the incredible challenges and opportunities we are facing in our communities and the world's cities. So, how can we improve our communities and thus the world, while also reaching out to the millions in need around the world?

World Vision, a Christian relief organization, answers the call of hungering and suffering peoples worldwide. Our son-in-law, Sam Jackson, has worked in this ministry for ten years. I have traveled with Sam to Ethiopia during the great famine and have witnessed what it is to be a good neighbor on a world scale.

Seeing Racism for What It Is

Racism is a problem that plagues many communities. It has certainly had its negative influence in our city of Los Angeles.

Tony Evans, well-known African-American evangelist in Dallas, in late 1996 delivered a powerful lesson on racism to a predominantly white, four-thousand-member church in Fort Worth. Rick Atchley, regular minister for the church, had just concluded a dynamic series of lessons on that same topic, during which time he and Tony had become friends.

Tony's primary message was, "Racism is not a social issue; it's a spiritual issue. It isn't a cultural problem; it's sin."

Tony pointed out that racially segregated congregations are one of the biggest failings of the church. They are in direct opposition to Jesus' prayer for unity in John 17 where he says in verse 21, "Father, I pray that they can be one . . . then the world will believe that you sent me."

In other words, segregated Christians give the wrong message to our neighbors and communities. We don't present a unified picture that helps to overcome the sin of racism. Rather, we perpetuate racial division and disunity, even within the church.

But community racism isn't just a black-and-white issue. It's a red-and-yellow-brown-and-beige issue too. It involves all races and all communities. Tony remarked, "We should not be ashamed of the gospel of the church of all races." And we should work aggressively to bring the good message of unity to our neighbors and friends by being unified ourselves. Let them see that we love each other, no matter what color or culture we are. That's the church the Lord built, and that's a big step forward in moving our towns and cities from problems to peace.

> "Racism is not a social issue; it's a spiritual issue. It's not a cultural problem; it's sin."

Enrich Your Community

One of the most amazing people I know of is Jan Johnson. She worked tirelessly for eight years to unite people, churches, businesses, government agencies, and civic organizations into a giant financial and volunteer support group, which is now the largest nonprofit housing program for the homeless in our nation—the Adopt-a-Family program of the Community Enrichment Center in North Richland Hills, Texas.

This wonderful center annually feeds thirty thousand people, houses hundreds of homeless families, provides clothing for them, sponsor's a job bank to help them get back on their feet, and offers counseling in areas of need.

In 1987, with little money and a big vision, Jan began recruiting people, money, sponsors, food, and clothes from every source she could imagine to help the hungry and homeless in north central

Texas. One day at a time, the program grew. People volunteered their time, businesses gave money and goods, and counselors counseled. Day by day more and more hurting people were helped. Soon the program outgrew its facilities.

> "Let each of us please our neighbors for their good, to help them be stronger in faith."

Every week the Community Enrichment Center receives an eighteen-wheel truckload of staple foods and groceries to be redistributed to the hungry. And that's just from one sponsor. Combined with other corporate sponsors and donors of all kinds, soon there was so much food being brought to the center that some of it was having to be left outside for a day or two because there was just no more room for it.

In 1993 Jan proposed to her board of directors that a new facility be built. It would cost about $650,000. Now, saying no to Jan Johnson is like telling Uncle Sam that you really wouldn't care to be drafted. At her challenge, and based on her reputation for doing good in the community, major foundations began making matching grants to the center, and by the middle of 1994, Jan had raised over $700,000. In 1995 the Community Enrichment Center opened new facilities that now help three times as many destitute families as before. And it was paid for *in advance* by people who believe in the power of good over evil in their community. Jan Johnson lives daily the command of Romans 15:2: "Let each of us please our neighbors for their good, to help them be stronger in faith."

OPEN ARMS HOME

From the Adopt-a-Family program emerged a second, more specific program called Open Arms Home, Inc. This outreach effort provides interim housing, jobs, counseling, food, clothes, and support for abused women and children. For a two-year period, Open Arms provides a safe, rent-free home where clients can find emotional and physical healing. When they have reestablished themselves as confident, self-supporting citizens, Open Arms has a graduation celebration, which often includes allowing them to purchase the home they have been using. What a great program!

Jan has now moved into a new dimension of service. She provides seminars and training for people, organizations, and churches nationwide who want to start their own programs of relief like Adopt-a-Family and/or Open Arms. In this way, the outreach can expand much more quickly, and the power of good will be felt throughout the country. (See the Resources and Opportunities for Good appendix for more information.)

That's what I call enriching your community! And it can be done in any community by people just like Jan who are committed to defeating evil by doing good.

MAKE-A-DIFFERENCE DAY

Captain Scott O'Grady has experienced firsthand the profound impact of helping someone in need. When his F-16 was shot down over Bosnia in June 1995, the U.S. Air Force captain ejected into the desert and was suddenly a national hero.

He survived in hostile territory for six days and nights by eating insects and grass and drinking rainwater. Everyone thought he was dead, until Captain Thomas Hanford, a member of the search crew, heard him respond to his radio call sign, "Basher 52."

Scott said, "I felt goose bumps all over, electricity rushing through me. I wanted to laugh and scream and cry and jump for joy, everything short of an Irish jig. Hanford had been flying all night and was finished with his schedule. But he had extra gas and could stay out another ten to twenty minutes. He could have gone home. I'm *really* happy he didn't go home."

As a result of Captain Hanford's extra effort, Scott was picked up in a dramatic daylight rescue. And he came home with a new resolve to put more balance in his life: "to take better care of myself and to do as much as I could for others."

Make-a-Difference-Day is one of the ways Scott tries to help others, out of gratitude for the way he was helped. This effort magnifies what people can do for their communities. It's not just one small local effort, but many communities connected throughout the entire nation. That's big. And it's very positive.

You can do so many goods things on Make-a-Difference Day. A community improvement, such as picking up trash or removing graffiti or planting flowers and trees in the park, is so positive. Is there a city fence that needs repairing or painting? Could your civic club join Adopt-a-Highway and clean up a mile of highway that leads into your town? Perhaps your church could spend the day helping the homeless or doing a cleanup-fix-up project for elderly people. Why not take a youth group on a tree-planting day?

Look around you. There must be dozens of ways you and your friends and family can make a difference in your city for one day or, even better, on an ongoing basis.

For information on how to get involved with Make-a-Difference Day, refer to the Resources and Opportunities for Good appendix.

IMPACT LOCAL POLITICS

Many people feel ineffective when it comes to participating in politics. We read so much about corruption and see so many dishonest and manipulating politicians that we often think we're defeated before we even begin.

But wait! I believe that anything that has gone wrong can go right again—even in politics. Here are three simple-but-effective ways you can help make the politics and politicians in your city "go right" again.

1. Coordinate a voter-registration drive. Target neighborhoods in your city where voter turnout has been low in the past. Mobilize a group of workers to go door to door and sign up voters—

young people, retired people, a civic group, a church group. The broader the scope of voters, the more accurately an election will reflect the will of all the people in town. Contact your voter-registration office for sign-up regulations and supplies.

2. Work in an election campaign. You don't have to be a genius to stuff envelopes and hand out posters for a candidate for office. Carefully choose a candidate you feel is upholding goodness and decency, and help him or her get elected. Answer the telephone, make badges, hang banners. Do whatever is needed to help the right candidate end up in an influential position in town.

3. Take your local representatives to lunch. Get to know the people who are making decisions for you and your family. Let them get to know you and your political beliefs and wishes for good government. Don't assume that they really know what all their constituents want them to do while they are in office. They need input from you if you want them to represent you correctly.

Distribute Good Literature

A great way to affect your community for good is with a personal literature campaign. One of my favorite tracts is called "Someone Died and Left You a Fortune." It's a small, single-fold tract that briefly explains God's grace and offer of salvation. On the back it has a place to put your address and/or phone number or, perhaps, the phone number of your church. I personally keep a copy of the devotional guide, *Power for Today*, in my pocket to give away.

Keep a few tracts that you like in your purse or pocket. Here are some aggressive-but-nice ways to use them:

- Leave them with your tips on the tables in restaurants where you dine.
- Hand one to the driver when you get off the bus.
- Put some in the literature racks at the bus station, airport, or train station.

- Mail one with each household bill when you pay it.
- Give one to any person who comes to your door selling something.
- Hand one to the checker at the grocery store when you leave.
- Give one to the attendant at the cleaners.
- Give one to the person working the window when you go through a drive-through restaurant.
- Hand one to the bank teller, or send it in through the chute with your deposit.
- Leave some on the tables in waiting rooms of doctors, dentists, attorneys, and other professionals when you're in their offices.
- Post them on information bulletin boards in public places.

There must be literally hundreds of ways you can aggressively distribute tasteful tracts to people without being pushy or offensive. And you never know what impact they might have. Try it! "Doing what is right makes a nation great" (Proverbs 14:34).

THE PARENT INSTITUTE

In our city of Los Angeles, a community program has been designed to involve parents in their children's learning. It's a cooperative effort with World Vision, the Los Angeles Unified School District, Los Angeles Annenberg Metropolitan Project (LAAMP), and LEARN.

Since the program's start in April 1992, over 47,906 parents have completed the nine-week course. Another 45,000 parents have graduated from similar programs within San Diego County, Orange County, and the Bay Area. And the results are excellent, as demonstrated in this family's story.

A man who works as a welder and his wife have six children. These parents were concerned about their children and wanted to see them do well in life. The mother was told by her neighbors that she was too poor and uneducated to expect her children to make much progress, but she didn't agree.

So, in the mid-1980s they attended the Parent Institute course and "the light went on." She suddenly realized that she could influence her children to go to college.

Now, ten years later, five of her children have graduated from college, and one is still in school. One is studying to be a minister and another one is working on a doctorate.

In 1996 these six children gave their parents an extended European vacation to thank them for inspiring them and helping them to succeed beyond what their original social situation predicted.

This is only one of many success stories from the Parent Institute—a program that can be established in most any city or community. For information about this program, refer to the resource appendix.

SPIRITUAL OUTREACH TO THE DUMP

Midst rotted chicken pieces and soiled diapers, the poorest of the poor who live in one of Guatemala City's garbage dumps scavenge for scraps to eat. Into this decaying world came Gladys and Lisbeth, two Guatemalan women who traded their comfortable counseling careers for a spiritual outreach to the "dump people," according to Ana Gascon Ivey in an article titled "Down in the Dumps in Guatemala," in the July/August, 1994, issue of *Clarity* magazine.

"A lot of my friends thought I was crazy," remembers Gladys. "For a few years we didn't have any volunteers. I tried recruiting young people from my church, but a brother in the church told them not to help because of the danger. Others thought we'd catch a disease. People thought it was a phase and we'd get over it."

But Gladys and Lisbeth didn't get over it. Instead, they forged ahead, and the ministry burgeoned. It's often depressing and discouraging, but it's what they feel compelled to do and where they want to be. Both Gladys and Lisbeth receive invitations to teach or work with other ministries, but their hearts stay buried in the dump. These women can't envision their lives away from the *Casa de Alfarero's* needy landfill residents, and they dream about the people's futures.

"I ask the Lord to not let me die until I see spiritual revival here," says Lisbeth. "We've been planting seeds for several years, and I would like to see the [people] seek the Lord sincerely. That is my desire, to see a spiritual revival here, because I know that's the exit to their pain and suffering. When we don't see changes, we still must maintain obedience to God. The Lord calls us to plant and bless, independent of results."

✧

"When we don't see changes, we still must maintain obedience to God."

✧

People should never be left in the dump, whether it's a physical dump or a spiritual dump. They are precious souls, not just vacant bodies. They are as important to the God who made them as we are. He hears their aching sobs in the night and wants to reach out to comfort and care for them like the gentle Father he is. Their tears trickle down his cheeks. Their pain seers through his heart. Their fears haunt his mind.

When he looks around his world to find someone to send to the dump to help his children, will Gladys and Lisbeth be the only two servants he can find? Or will we go and help our neighbors—our brothers and sisters in the dump?

Another example comes from Honduras where our friend, Doris Clark, a widow, directs and promotes a remarkable ministry to the poor. Far from the big cities, her ministry is located on an inaccessible mountain. She operates a Christian medical clinic, an alcohol-treatment clinic using the twelve steps, and an extensive food-distribution program. The president of Honduras complimented her to me in extravagant terms. Her motivation is Matthew 25:40: "Anything you did for even the least of my people here, you also did for me."

UNION RESCUE MISSION

Lyman Stewart, founder of Union Oil Company, possessed a great missionary zeal. He supported it with his talent for finding oil, his wildcat fervor, and a heart motivated to benefit mankind. Through all of his success and wealth, he never lost sight of his dream of becoming a servant of mankind.

Stewart and his friend, Major Hilton, joined a group of earnest evangelical leaders at a local YMCA to discuss relief programs for the hurting and homeless in a section of Los Angeles called Skid Row. And on December 4, 1891, Union Rescue Mission was established. It has been reaching out to the street people on the Pacific coast ever since.

As a member of the board of directors for the mission, I am always humbled by the people I meet there, both the helpers and those being helped. The mission has served as a combination relief society, employment bureau, restaurant, hotel, and a place to "rehabilitate human derelicts who have been wrecked by the storms of life," as Helga Bender Henry wrote in her book, *Mission on Main Street*.

"The mission," she wrote, "is a spiritual awakener, a crime preventer, a soul-saving institution . . . where men are changed from liabilities to assets."

In his introduction to a more recent book about the mission, titled *Accomplishing Union Rescue's Mission* (self-published by the mission), its president, Warren Currie, said this:

> I am intrigued about the place Jesus, when on earth, called home. He lived in Capernaum, a town peopled by transients and migrants, bordering Damascus. Isaiah described Capernaum as a land of Gentiles and a land of

death. It was the place where Jesus healed the lepers, outcasts who made their home in that area. The poor found shelter there, and they were his choice of neighbors.

Our guests come with every imaginable disease. Respiratory illness from sleeping on the cold cement is rampant. HIV continues to increase. Our location is a Jesus location. We are in the "Capernaum" section of Los Angeles. We do as he did by following his example to recover sight for the blind, offer relief through the medical center, and spiritual sight through his unchanging message, one life at a time.

Our release of the oppressed is best witnessed in the family arena where women and children find safety. One woman, raped three times in a single day, redefined oppression. Today she walks in newness of life . . . Here oppression resolves into opportunity.

Union Rescue Mission is a great example, in my opinion, of what good neighbors and a spirit of community are all about. I am proud to be part of its ongoing work and dream. Perhaps you could be the spark to light the candle of mission on the streets of your community. All fires begin with one tiny spark.

Community service and outreach can take many different forms. It can be anything from planting trees to rescuing people from the streets or the dump. The point is to do something . . . anything . . . that will cause the light of God to shine in your city and town for good. Don't leave it to the people down the street, the civic groups, the church groups, or the elected officials. Don't wait for city ordinances to be passed. Don't sit around and hope for a miracle to zap away the dilapidated buildings and weed-infested parks. Instead, get out your paint brush and your lawn mower and lend a helping hand. Help the spiritually and physically needy where you are today.

George L. Graziadio, founder of the Imperial Bank for whom the George L. Graziadio School of Business and Management at Pepperdine University is named, has a favorite term: TNT, which translates

CHAPTER TEN

For God Alone Is Good

secret

No. 10 – Let your life be a reflection of the light of God—the creator and source of all good—so that all who see your good deeds will glorify him.

Dr. Richard Mouw

President,
Fuller Theological Seminary

God in Jesus Christ is working out his purposes in the world. It is not obvious that he is doing so. But he is. And he has not left us without a witness. From the community that exists under his direct authority, he sends us forth to confront the thrones and dominions and principalities and authorities that he has created and that are held together by him. We are not left alone to act without guidance. For the one who has created those powers and who holds them together is the one who sends us forth to declare his marvelous works in their presence.

The Lord is pleased with a good person,
but he will punish anyone who plans evil.

Proverbs 12:2

The Powerful Source of All Good

W e should have stopped sailing when we originally planned. But it was so easy to forget our worries on the sparkling Pacific, and we both needed an afternoon's escape.

Pepperdine had been going through some difficult times. We had recently opened our new Malibu Beach campus, and we had kept our old one going in Los Angeles near the Watts area. Now we were beginning to wonder if we could operate both successfully. We had money problems, administrative problems, problems everywhere. So I was glad when my friend, Bill Banowsky, our university president, suggested we take out the fourteen-foot catamaran.

Near sunset we came back to shore, beached the catamaran, and returned to our driftwood fire. Over the darkening Pacific, the wind was picking up. Bill looked at me, a glint in his eyes, and I knew what he had in mind.

"Great!" I said. "One more time."

Together we began to push the light craft down the sand toward the water. The catamaran is a cat-rigged sailboat composed of two long metal pontoons, which support a raised deck of canvas capable of holding two or three people. Because of its unique design, the craft slices through the water with exceptional speed and power.

As we slid the boat into the water, I was pushing on the starboard side, and Bill was standing at the stern. The surf foamed at our waists, and we prepared to hoist ourselves onto the canvas deck.

Suddenly, the wind caught the sail and snapped it with the sound of a rifle crack. The boat shot forward like a bullet. I managed to grab the stern of the starboard pontoon and was instantly yanked off my feet. I found myself being dragged out to sea.

Bill lunged forward, trying to catch the boat, but he was left behind. The last I saw of him was his shocked face as he screamed, "Climb on!" But, as the craft surged out to sea, I felt as if I were being dragged behind a runaway locomotive. I unsuccessfully tried to climb on board. Now it was too late to let go because the distance to shore was far greater than my swimming endurance.

As I was dragged along, the powerful water pressure pulled my pants off right over my shoes. I hung on, arms stretched before me, trying to keep my head above water. The ocean was icy, and my body was fast becoming numb.

I tried to pull myself up on the pontoon, but try as I might, I couldn't lift myself even six inches. The racing water held me down and back. Panic filled me. This mindless craft would race on endlessly, towing me like some infuriated whale.

I tried to climb onto the pontoon again, but fell back gasping. My arms were weakening, pain shot through my elbows and shoulders. How long could I hang on?

Alone under the darkening sky with only the roar of foaming water in my ears, I knew I faced death. How ironic, I thought, when only minutes before I had been warming myself contentedly by the beach fire and discussing the university's problems with Bill.

My thoughts turned to Helen and the children. "Oh, God, help me, help me!" I gasped. "Give me strength to hang on."

My arms were like wood. I couldn't feel through my hands any more. Once more. Just once more. I called on my last remaining strength and threw a leg over the pontoon. Pain seared through me as the back of my knee struck a sharp metal projection, and blood ran down my leg. I slipped back deeper into the churning water, coughing and choking.

I was now at least two miles from shore. Even if a search was sent out, I despaired of anyone finding me in that vast ocean. Soon my hands would slip from the cold metal pontoon, and I would sink into the ocean depths, like a sailor buried at sea.

Now the waves increased in size, and I lost all hope as the cold, foaming breakers crashed down on me. So many times I had told others that "God is our protection and our strength. He always helps in times of trouble" (Psalm 46:1), but now my faith was weak, and I was terrified.

"Oh, God, help me, help me," I continued praying as the surging catamaran pitched in the rolling waves. Over and over those words flooded my heart.

✧

I lost all hope as the cold, foaming breakers crashed down on me.

✧

Then, as if prompted by something deep within me, my panicky feeling suddenly evaporated, leaving me able to study my enemy, the ocean waves. Until now, I had not been able to conquer my fear long enough to really look at how to combat it. I saw now that each time the bow of the catamaran rose to meet a big wave, my end of the pontoon was momentarily buried in the water.

I awaited my opportunity. Here came another wave . . . there! I had managed to hoist my leg over the pontoon.

Now wait. Here came another green, crashing roller. Quick, lift!

By using the waves, I had been able to shift more of my body out of the water. With each wave I was able to get more of me onto the pontoon. To my spent energy, God had added his power. Finally I lay on top of the boat's surface, hugging the cold metal, breathing hard. I looked up. The twenty-five-mile-per-hour wind was still driving us out to sea. It would be impossible to crawl forward to the tiller, but I could reach the rod guiding the rudder!

I shoved it as hard as I could, forcing the craft to turn toward shore. As she came about, the wind caught the sail with such enormous force that the boat capsized. But at least she was now dead in the water. I rolled onto the flat side of the exposed pontoon and lay there exhausted. "Thank you, God," I kept saying with every breath.

After a while I heard a faint voice calling: "Hang on, brother . . . hang on." Bill and his son had commandeered a neighbor's boat and had come out to rescue me. I lay on the deck as we returned to shore; I was shivering cold, but my heart was singing songs of praise.

I have since thought of the many lessons I learned that day.

Lessons Learned

RESPECT THE POWER OF THE ENEMY

The first lesson I learned was a greater respect for the power of the ocean, which was my temporary enemy. (I should have taken our university course in sailing before venturing out!) Before nearly being swallowed alive by the ocean, I had only an intellectual respect and fear for it. I knew that it could be dangerous and that other people had lost their lives to it. But like most people without firsthand experience, I didn't really believe it could happen to me . . . until it almost did.

In a similar way, most Christians seem to have only a passive respect for their mortal enemy, the devil. Of course, we know intellectually that Satan is evil and that the Bible teaches us to beware of his dangerous deceptions. Still, it seems that we don't give him the fearful respect he deserves. Many Christians don't believe that Satan is real. Because they don't think of him running down their street in a red suit and carrying a pitchfork, they think of him as a fairy tale.

If the devil were a flood, we would be out furiously sandbagging the riverbank to keep him from running through our homes with death and destruction.

If the devil were a hurricane, we would be out frantically boarding up the windows and doors to keep his winds from ripping our lives apart.

✧

Good on the offense will always put evil on the defense.

✧

Instead, the devil uses our television sets, newspapers, and magazines. And when he attacks us in our own living rooms with violence, extramarital sex, pornography, nudity, and perverse language, we may simply yawn and go back to sleep in our recliners.

The devil uses money. And we greedily try to stuff our pockets full of it. We horde it as our very own and keep it selfishly for ourselves. We work ourselves into exhaustion for it. We trust in it and believe it can protect us and give us security. We foolishly fall in love with it.

The devil uses fame and position. We step on other people to get to it. We clamor for attention and do whatever is necessary to possess it.

In truth, we don't always have fearful respect for the devil's power. And, just like the ocean, one day he may swallow us up because we are not prepared to fight him off. We must learn to use the light of Christ to defeat his evil attacks.

Never underestimate the evil that Satan can do. Give him no small entrance into your life. Offer him no olive branch. He has no redeeming features. He is the enemy, and he will never be anything else.

At the same time, never underestimate the power of good in defeating him. Good on the offense will always put evil on the defense.

LIVE WITH JOY AND THANKSGIVING

The second lesson I learned while being dragged through the sea is a deep resolve to live every day with a sense of joy and thanksgiving. It's great to be alive! And every day offers us the chance to praise God for his amazing grace and salvation.

I was never more thankful for anything in my life than to be rescued from the icy Pacific. Bill's voice from his rescue boat was the sweetest sound. It represented hope and life. It drove away the darkness I felt in my heart. It was beautiful!

All I could think to say was, "Thank you, God. Thank you, God. Oh, thank you, God!" I knew that he was the source of my hope and salvation, just as he is for people who are lost in the depths of sin today. He is the Light of hope and life. He can drive the darkness out of their hearts and minds. He is beautiful! He is marvelous! He alone is good.

APPRECIATE GOD MORE DEEPLY

The third lesson I learned from that overturned catamaran was a deeper appreciation of our God, who hears and answers in times of trouble. I'll never forget Bill calling out to me: "Hang on, brother, hang on!" God had heard my cries in the night. He had given his strength to me when I needed it most. He had been the lighthouse that led Bill to me through the darkness. He had rescued me when I couldn't save myself. He had come when I called.

God saved my life from physical danger, just as he will deliver those in spiritual danger who call to him from their deep need. Through Christians he calls out to them, "Hang on! Don't give up. I'm coming. Hang on!"

USE PROBLEMS TO OVERCOME PROBLEMS

My experience in the sea also taught me that I should not be overcome with my problems and that I should see the bigger picture and know that God has a solution. Out there on the waves, I discovered a profound truth: the danger I thought would destroy me—those angry, engulfing waves—when studied in the calmness of the Spirit, proved to be my very opportunity of escape, once I saw how to use it.

In those fearful moments, God taught me that there is a way to victory over human problems, if we place ourselves completely in his hands. We must learn to use the waves to win over the waves.

How does that translate into everyday life? It means that we must use good health habits to overcome bad health. We must use the media itself in an aggressively good way to overcome the potential evil of the media. We must use the power of good words to defeat the effects of bad communication. We must overcome the problems in our communities by using community facilities and organizations to effect those changes. We must replace victimized thinking with victorious thinking.

Whatever Satan would use for evil, we must use for good instead. We have to stay one step ahead of him.

Carry the Torch

The early Christians held up the light and carried it through the dark streets of the world, like those who carry the Olympic torch. They were persecuted for their faith, but they were willing to suffer so that others could be saved.

Tradition has it that every one of the writers of the New Testament died for the Light. Matthew was beheaded. Mark was dragged through the streets of Alexandria by a team of wild horses until he died. Luke was hanged from the branch of an olive tree, Paul was beheaded, Peter and Jude were crucified, James was beaten to death with a club, and John was banished to the Isle of Patmos, where he spent his old age in isolation. And these are not the only ones who have kept the light burning brightly through the ages.

Paul Marshall has just completed a powerful book titled *Their Blood Cries Out*, which exposes and documents incredible worldwide persecution of Christians today. It's eye-opening for any Christian. While we know very little of vicious physical persecution in America, there are thousands of Christians who are being tormented and terrorized in many countries. We cannot say that physical persecution will not come to America, but if it should come and we respond in unmovable faith, we have this promise from God: "You have a great reward waiting for you in heaven. People did the same evil things to the prophets who lived before you" (Matthew 5:12).

The light of God never shines so brightly as in the eyes of his persecuted saints and martyrs. And the power of that light astounds the perpetrators of evil.

Recognize the Power of the Light

Jesus said in John 9:15, "While I am in the world, I am the light of the world." And that light was so powerful that it had dramatic effects on the people it touched:

- When the light was born into the world, its power was demonstrated as a brilliant new star in the eastern sky. Cruel Herod was so terrified by the reports of the light that he tried to have it extinguished, but to no avail. The light shone so brightly that kings and princes have bowed before it down through the ages.

- When Saul of Tarsus was on the road to Damascus to find Christians and persecute them (Acts 9), the brilliance and power of the light knocked him to the ground and blinded him. Then the power of the light converted persecuting Saul into saintly Paul, who carried the light into the darkness of the Gentile world.

- When the Roman soldiers came to arrest Jesus in the Garden of Gethsemane and faced the light, its power knocked them to the ground (John 18:6). They couldn't stand up to it; their evil was overwhelmed by its beauty and goodness.

- John the apostle was taken up into heaven where he saw the light among the seven golden lampstands. He says in Revelation 1:17, "When I saw him, I fell down at his feet like a dead man." He fainted from the power of the light. Even his goodness was as evil compared to the light of the Son of God.

In truth, nothing could resist the light of the world. The light ascended into heaven, but we were not left to fend for ourselves in the darkness. Listen to what Jesus told his followers about the light:

> *You* are the light that gives light to the world. A city that is built on a hill cannot be hidden. And people don't hide a light under a bowl. They put it on a lampstand so the light shines for all the people in the house. In the same way, *you* should be a light for other people. *Live so that they will see the good things you do* and will praise your Father in heaven. (Matthew 5:14–16, emphasis mine)

As long as true Christians are in the world, Jesus is in the world, and the light of the world shines as brightly as ever through "the good things you do."

Serve as Reflectors and Refractors

When we do the good things that Jesus did, we reflect the light to the world. When we say the good things that Jesus said, we reflect the light. When we teach as he taught, live as he lived, and touch others as he touched others with gentleness and compassion, we reflect the light into the dark corners of the world.

It's not that we are the light in and of ourselves, rather, we let his light shine through us into the lives of people around us. And when they see us live as he lived, "they will praise your Father in heaven." Notice, it does not say, "they will praise *you*."

It's like a mirror. When you see a beautiful girl in a mirror, you don't say, "Wow! What a great mirror." You say, "Wow! What a beautiful girl." And when people see God's goodness through us, they won't praise us, but him. Our task is to keep the mirror clean and clear so that his image is sharp and true.

In addition to our being *reflectors* of God's light, we are also *refractors* of his light. Through the myriad of talents and abilities God has given to Christians, we refract—or bend—the light to show all its beautiful colors and hues to the world. While one Christian refracts the light through preaching, another does so through singing, and another does it through service to the poor. Some Christians refract the light through a jail ministry, others through teaching in private or public schools, and others through feeding the hungry. The ways are endless, and the light shines brilliantly through each one—now red, now yellow, now blue, now green. And that's exactly the way God intended it to be.

What talents and abilities has he given to you for refracting the light to the world around you? Are you a carpenter, a seamstress, an accountant, or caregiver? Did he bless you with culinary skills, the ability to fix broken things, or the gift of encouragement? Perhaps your talent lies in gardening, leadership, medicine, law, making others laugh, or sales. Whatever your area of expertise—and we all have at least one—find a way to focus it on defeating evil with good.

Make My Day!

If we could honor God with one special day of our lives to truly glorify him, what would it be? "A *good* day," you say? Yes, no doubt. But what would that day be like? What things would we do to honor God and make his day? Isaiah tells us the Lord's answer:

> I will tell you the kind of special day I want:
> Free the people you have put in prison unfairly
>   and undo their chains.
> Free those to whom you are unfair
>   and stop their hard labor.
> Share your food with the hungry

and bring poor, homeless people
into your own homes.

When you see someone who has no clothes,
give him yours,
and don't refuse to help your own relatives.
Then your light will shine like the dawn,
and your wounds will quickly heal.
Your God will walk before you,
and the glory of the Lord will protect you
. from behind.
Then you will call out, and the Lord will answer.
You will cry out, and he will say, "Here I am."

If you stop making trouble for others,
if you stop using cruel words and pointing
your finger at others,
if you feed those who are hungry
and take care of the needs
of those who are troubled,
then your light will shine in the darkness,
and you will be bright like sunshine at noon.
(Isaiah 58:6–10)

The Lord says, "Do good, and I will walk before you to clear your way." And a little later, in Isaiah 60:1–3, he goes on to say:

Get up and shine because your light has come and
the glory of the Lord shines on you.
Darkness now covers the earth;
deep darkness covers her people.
But the Lord shines on you,
and people see his glory around you.
Nations will come to your light;
kings will come to the brightness of your
sunrise.

When we shine as we are meant to shine, the world will see the light and come to it. But how can they respond if the light fails to shine?

Do What You Were Created to Do

Reflecting and refracting the light to the world is not just a sideline of the Christian life. Doing good works is not something we are meant to do in our spare time. It's not a hobby or a pastime. It's what we were *created to do:* "God has made us what we are. In Christ Jesus, God made us to do good works, which God planned in advance for us to live our lives doing" (Ephesians 2:10).

God didn't create us just to make money. He didn't create us to be famous or infamous. He didn't plan for us to spend our lives chasing after finite earthly dreams. He created us "to do good works" and thus glorify him. That's our purpose. That's his plan and goal for us. Doing good works is what he knows will make us happy, joyful people. God knows that doing good adds zest and delight to life. It takes away the doldrums and gives meaning to everyday living.

✧

If the light stops shining, the world will crash into total darkness.

✧

So, will doing good works save us? Is that why we do them? No. Christians have already been saved by the grace of God through our faith and obedience (Ephesians 2:8). That's what made us "new people." But because we have now been saved, it's a natural response for us, as new people, to do good works to express our gratitude to him and because we want other people to be saved as well.

The Bible describes hell as a place of utter darkness. It is a place that is devoid of the light of God. In 2 Peter 2:17, Peter says that false teachers have "a place in the blackest darkness" being kept for them. And the Lord has kept the angels who turned against him "in darkness . . . bound with everlasting chains" (Jude 6). Is it any wonder, then, that we sometimes hear people who are lost describe life as "hell on earth?" They are without the light of God.

Christians are children of the light. Jesus has ascended into heaven and left us in charge of the lighthouse. If it stops shining, the world will crash into total darkness, like a ship crashing into the rocks along the shore.

Know the Source of Good

Good does not start with man, but with God, for "only God is good" (Mark 10:18). Anything good that happens is of God. The Old Testament emphasizes that God is the source of all good, the creator and sustainer of every man and every impulse for good in each one of us. It teaches that his love for us is eternal, and it points throughout to someone who is to come.

When Jesus came to earth, he revealed God to us completely, so that we could understand God better by seeing him in human form. He is *Emmanuel*—God with us. And our God in human form "went everywhere doing good" (Acts 10:38). Jesus was, in his very nature, God himself. Jesus was God's perfect example of what he wants us to be, and he "went everywhere doing good." He demonstrated to us the way to have a happy, fulfilling, and meaningful life; he "went everywhere doing good." In fact, according to John 21:25, if all the good things he did were written down in books, there would be so many that the world couldn't hold them.

Good is supremely demonstrated in Jesus—in how he lived, in what he taught, and in his resurrection. He didn't organize a protest against Rome. He didn't gather an army to overthrow slavery or other injustices. He didn't rain down fire from heaven to destroy his enemies or have a legion of angels sweep through the land to eradicate evil. He simply did good works everywhere he went.

He promised to build his church in such a way that hell itself could not withstand it. When we look at that church and see how small and weak it seemed to be, we know that the power of God was involved, or it would not have survived. And when we look at the power of the Roman civilization at that time and see the coliseum and other arenas where gladiators fought Christians to amuse the populace, or where Christians were mangled by wild animals for the entertainment of Roman royalty, we know what a powerful, evil force it was. And yet, the early church grew rapidly, in spite of and because of persecution. Their goodness overpowered the forces of evil. Notice how those early Christians are described in this anonymous "Letter to Diognetus," which possibly dates from the second century:

Those Christians

For Christians are not differentiated from other people by country, language, or customs; you see, they do not live in cities of their own, or speak some strange dialect, or have some peculiar lifestyle.

This teaching of theirs has not been contrived by the invention and speculation of inquisitive men; nor are they propagating mere human teaching as some people do. They live in both Greek and foreign cities, wherever chance has put them. They follow local customs in clothing, food, and the other aspects of life. But at the same time, they demonstrate to us the wonderful and certainly unusual form of their own citizenship.

They live in their own native lands, but as aliens; as citizens, they share all things with others; but like aliens, suffer all things. Every foreign country is to them as their native country, and every native land as a foreign country.

They marry and have children just like everyone else; but they do not kill unwanted babies. They offer a shared table, but not a shared bed. They are at present "in the flesh," but they don't live "according to the flesh." They are passing their days on earth, but are citizens of heaven. They obey the appointed laws, and go beyond the laws in their own lives.

They love everyone, but are persecuted by all. They are unknown and condemned; they are put to death and gain life. They are poor and yet make many rich. They are short of everything and, yet, have plenty of all things. They are dishonored and, yet, gain glory through dishonor.

Their names are blackened and, yet, they are cleared. They are mocked and bless in return. They are treated outrageously and behave respectfully to others. When they do good, they are punished as evildoers; when punished, they rejoice as if being given new life. They are attacked by Jews as aliens, and are persecuted by Greeks; yet those who hate them cannot give any reason for their hostility.

To put it simply—the soul is to the body as Christians are to the world. The soul is spread through all parts of the body and Christians through all the cities of the world. The soul is in the body but is not of the body; Christians are in the world but not of the world.

✧

Those Christians are our spiritual ancestors. When we finally have our great family reunion on the Day of Judgment, will they be as proud to call us relatives as we are to claim them? Will those who record our history have anything worthwhile to say about Christians today that even slightly compares to this letter? Perhaps so, if we follow the direction of 1 Thessalonians 5:21–22: "Test everything. Keep what is good, and stay away from everything that is evil."

"They have children like everyone else, but they do not kill unwanted babies."

✧

201

Let Your Light Shine

Samuel Morse, inventor of the telegraph, was once asked by a friend, "Professor, when you were making your experiments, did you ever come to a place of not knowing what to do next?"

"More than once," responded Morse, "and whenever I couldn't see my way clearly, I knelt down and prayed to God for light and understanding."

Then Morse said, "When flattering honors came to me from America and Europe on account of my invention, I never felt I deserved them. I had made valuable application of electricity, not because I was superior to other men, but solely because God, who meant it for mankind, must reveal it to someone, and was pleased to reveal it to me."

In May 1844 the first message to be sent over the telegraph, dispatched by Morse himself between Washington and Baltimore, were these words: "What hath God wrought!"

I know that some people are cynical about the future. They believe that Satan's forces of evil will overcome God's forces of good, but don't be one of them! I stand on tiptoe to look over the horizon and see what God has in store for you and me in the years ahead. I think of the words of Joshua 3:5, when Joshua challenged the children of Israel before they marched into the Promised Land: "Make yourselves holy, because tomorrow the Lord will do amazing things among you."

God has done mighty wonders among us in the years that have passed. He has healed the dying, helped the helpless, forgiven the vilest sinners, encouraged the spiritually weak, and loved each of us just as we are. But I believe he has even greater things in store for

✧

"I stand on tiptoe to look over the horizon and see what God has in store for you and me in the years ahead."

✧

202

us in the future. By faith I face tomorrow with e
has given us a task, and we must fulfill it. We ar
the world.

We are the keepers of the lighthou
sure that the light always shines! Even thoug
seem like only a flickering candle in a sea of da
keep it shining. "In the same way, you should
people. Live so that they . . . will praise you
(Matthew 5:16).

We are the voice of joy and hope
wilderness crying, "Prepare the way [for the
clear for my people" (Isaiah 57:14). He brings s

We are the trumpet of the Lord, a
fare the coming of the Lord of light in all his
Lord Jesus!

We are the bread of life for our spirit
Without us to share it with them, they will die.

We are the compassion of Jesus. W
through his tear-brimmed eyes, we hear with hi
ror in the night, and we run with his legs to co

who
evil

We are the keys to the kingdom of
open the gates to allow entrance to the lonely, th

We are the light of the world. Indiv
ering candles, but together we are the noond
and health and hope to people everywhere. W
us alone is entirely possible for us through him.
Notes wrote, "You are the light of the world if .

FOR GOD ALONE IS GOOD

You are a quiet doer of good,
>> rather than a noisy complainer
>> about evil;

You are feeding one hungry person,
>> rather than lamenting world hunger;

You are keeping your own neighborhood
>> streets and sidewalks clean,
>> rather than grumbling about the city's
>> litter and graffiti;

You are an informed voter,
>> rather than a nonvoting curser of
>> government corruption;

You are praying for peace,
>> rather than decrying the evils
>> of war;

You are upgrading your child's school,
>> rather than degrading the
>> educational system;

You are an aggressive part of the solution,
>> rather than a passive part of the
>> problem.

member that God is the source of all good, and he is the one
ave us this challenge: "Do not let evil defeat you, but defeat
doing good" (Romans 12:21).

BENEDICTION

✧

May the Lord Bless You

As this book is released, I pray that the Lord may bless you with more faith, more hope, more joy, and more love for God and all people. I pray that the light of good will glow brightly in your life, that your faith will express itself in aggressive goodness, that cynicism and despair will not be allowed to blow out your candle, and that God will be glorified in your life.

It is my humble hope that this book may somehow inspire you to do the will of God by becoming the reflected and refracted light of the world. Amen.

Resources and Opportunities for Good

Resources

Apple Blossoms
by Mary Hollingsworth
C. R. Gibson Co.
Norwalk, CT

Before Our Very Eyes
by Ronald A. Reno
Focus on the Family Publishing
8655 Explorer Drive
Colorado Springs, CO 80995
719-531-3400
Fax: 719-531-3484

Brain Builders! A Lifelong Guide to Sharper Thinking, Better Memory, and an Age-Proof Mind
by Richard Leviton
Parker Publishing Company
W. Nyack, NY

Christian News and Notes
12 East 48th St.
New York, NY 10017

Do What You Love, and the Money Will Follow
by J. Sinetar
Bantam Doubleday Dell Publishing Group, Inc.
1540 Broadway
New York, NY 10036

[Don't] Touch That Dial
by Barbara Hattemer and Robert Showers
Huntington House Publishers
PO Box 53788
Lafayette, LA 70505

Escape the Coming Night
by David Jeremiah with C. C. Carlson
Word Publishing
1501 LBJ Freeway, Suite 650
Dallas, TX 75234

Full Esteem Ahead: 100 Ways to Build Self-Esteem in Children and Adults
by Diane Loomans

Good Family Magazines
4050 Lee Vance View
Colorado Springs, CO 80918
719-531-7776
Fax: 719-535-0172

Guideposts
PO Box 1408
Carmel, NY 10512

Positive Living Magazine
Peale Center for Christian Living
66 East Main Street
Pawling, NY 12564
914-855-5000
Fax: 914-855-1462

Power for Today Magazine
(A Daily Devotional)
2809 Granny White Pike
Nashville, TN 37204
615-383-3842

Raising Faithful Kids in a Fast-Paced World
by Dr. Paul Faulkner
Howard Publishing
3117 N. 7th Street
West Monroe, LA 71291-2227
318-396-3122
Fax: 318-397-1882

Slouching towards Gomorrah
by Robert H. Bork
Regan Books, Harper-Collins
New York, NY

Taking on Donahue and TV Morality
by Richard Neill with Lela Gilbert
Multnomah Books/Questar Publishers
PO Box 1720
Sisters, OR 97759

The Chicago Manual of Style
The University of Chicago Press
Chicago, IL 60637

Their Blood Cries Out
by Paul Marshall with Lela Gilbert
Word Publishing
1501 BJ Freeway, Suite 650
Dallas, TX 75234

21st Century Christian Magazine
2809 Granny White Pike
Nashville, TN 37204
615-383-3842

WallBuilders, Inc.
PO Box 397
Aledo, TX 76008
817-441-6044

Vitality Magazine
Vitality, Incororated
8080 N. Central Expressway
Dallas, TX 75206

Opportunities

Adopt-a-Family
6300 NE Loop 820
Fort Worth, TX 76180
817-281-0773

Bread for a Hungry World
6300 NE Loop 820
North Richland Hills, TX 76180
817-281-0773
Fax: 817-281-8618
Web page: http:\\rhcc.metronet.com

Center for the Family
Pepperdine University
24255 Pacific Coast Highway
Malibu, CA 90263-4507
310-456-4000

Christian Higher Education Foundation
c/o Dr. John C. Stevens
Abilene Christian University
ACU Station
Abilene, TX 79699

John Templeton Foundation
c/o Ann Cameron
900 Can-Tex
Sewanee, TN 37375-2835

Joni and Friends, Inc.
PO Box 3333
28720 Canwood Street
Agoura Hills, CA 91301

Open Arms Home
6300 NE Loop 820
Fort Worth, TX 76180
817-281-0773

Promise Keepers
PO Box 103001
Denver, CO 80250-3001
303-964-7600

Resources for Living
2807 Manchaca
Austin, TX 78704
512-447-3607

The American Association for World Health
1825 K Street, N.W.
Suite 1208
Washington, DC 20006
202-466-5883

The National Coalition for Literacy
50 E. Huron Street
Chicago, IL 60611
312-280-3217

The Rutherford Institute
PO Box 7482
Charlottesville, VA 22906-7482
804-978-3888
Fax: 804-978-1789
E-mail: rutherford@fni.com

Union Rescue Mission
545 S. San Pedro St.
Los Angeles, CA 90013
213-457-6300

World Vision
220 I St., Ste. 270
Washington, DC 20002
800-777-5777

✦

Top-Ten Television Advertisers

The most influential allies in your efforts to improve television are the companies whose advertising dollars support TV programming. Listed below are the chairmen of the Top-Ten advertisers on network television. Feel free to write to them; they actually *want* to hear from you.

John E. Pepper, CEO
Procter & Gamble
Box 599
Cincinnati, OH 45201

John Smith
General Motors
3044 W. Grand Boulevard
Detroit, MI 48202

Geoffrey C. Bible
Philip Morris
120 Park Ave.
New York, NY 10017

Ralph S. Larsen
Johnson & Johnson
One J & J Plaza
New Brunswick, NJ 08933

Roger Enrico
PepsiCo
700 Anderson Hill Rd.
Purchase, NY 10577

Alex Trotman
Ford Motor Company
The American Road
Dearborn, MI 48121

Michael R. Quinlan
McDonald's
One McDonald's Plaza
Oak Brook, IL 60521

Arnold G. Langbo
Kellogg Company
One Kellogg Square
Battle Creek, MI 49016

Robert J. Eaton
Chrysler Corporation
1000 Chrysler Dr.
Auburn Hills, MI 48326